TYA: Essays on the Theatre for Young Audiences
by Moses Goldberg

anchorage press plays, inc.
applays.com
Louisville, Kentucky USA

Copyright ©2006
Moses Goldberg
All rights reserved

Cover Photograph by John Nation, *Louisville Magazine*
Book Design by Randy Blevins, jrbdesign
Printed by TCS, North Kansas City, MO.

Printed in the United States of America.
For information about permission to reproduce selections from this book contact the publisher, Anchorage Press Plays.

Anchorage Press Plays, Inc.
P.O. Box 2901
Louisville, KY 40201-2901 U.S.A.
www.applays.com

Chapter Eight reprinted with permission of the Children's Literature Association: Moses Goldberg, "The Child Audience: Toward a Theory of Aesthetic Development," *ChLA Quarterly* 9.3 (Fall 1984): 108-110.

ISBN 978-087602-039-5

ISBN 0-87602-039-2

For all the Children

TABLE OF CONTENTS

TYA: Essays on the Theatre for Young Audiences by Moses Goldberg

Contents

INTRODUCTION by Ben Cameron — page vii

PREFACE by Moses Goldberg — page x

THE POLITICS OF THEATRE FOR YOUNG AUDIENCES
1. Childhood, Education, and Society — page 3
2. On a National Arts Policy — page 12
3. The Three-Legged Stool — page 20
4. The 100% Audience — page 33
5. All Politics is Local — page 42
6. American Children's Theatre in the '80s — page 50

THE ART OF THEATRE FOR YOUNG AUDIENCES
7. On Ephemera — page 65
8. The Child Audience: Toward a Theory of Aesthetic Development — page 73
9. The Stage, by Stages — page 84
10. Participation Theatre — page 95
11. Stories and Storytellers — page 111
12. The Translator — page 122
13. The Actor/Priest — page 132
14. Riding the Tiger, or Instructions for the Actor — page 139
15. Pictures and Sounds — page 150

THE BUSINESS OF THEATRE FOR YOUNG AUDIENCES
16. The Chariot Driver — page 161
17. Two Audiences — page 171
18. The 60-Minute Myth — page 181
19. The Field Trip and the House Manager — page 192
20. The Next Wave — page 200

Introduction
by Ben Cameron

While theatre for young audiences (TYA) has long been recognized worldwide as one of the most vibrant and artistically creative components of the larger theatre field, we in the United States have been slow to recognize how truly essential TYA is. Thankfully, that is beginning to change. With the first ever Tony Award to a theatre for young audiences in 2003, the transfer of a TYA production to Broadway, and subsequent coverage in the national press, we are finally beginning to recognize that this is a field characterized at its best by boldness of artistry, and fearlessness of artists; it is a place where a specific kind of literacy and cultural citizenship are developed; and it is, for many, the entry point into a lifelong relationship with the arts.

These achievements could not be possible without the dedication and perseverance of a generation of pioneer practitioners—practitioners who often labored in the absence of serious critical coverage, significant philanthropic resources, and compensation commensurate with their achievements.

Among these pioneers is the inspiring Moses Goldberg, a man who has in particular emphasized the multiple functions theatre plays in the nurturing of larger cultural literacy and individual development—functions made possible when theatre thinks expansively beyond its traditional forms and invites active participation, not merely passive observation.

In the pages that follow, Moses offers the lessons of a lifetime in this field: practical observations about the performance event, financing, school relationships, and more. And yet this is more than an ambitious sequence of observations about the theatre, our economics, and our level (or often deficiencies) of achievement; it is a series of tart observations about our national cultural policy, our political process, our emerging national personality and more—all infused with both the frustrations that arise from laboring in a nation whose commitment to providing arts to our children is pallid at best and with the passions that spring from a lifetime of witnessing young lives transformed. It is a manifesto of sorts, stating emphatically those principles that Moses believes are essential if we are to move forward in this terrain—principles that will undoubtedly provoke agreement and dissension, discussion, and debate.

By stating these perspectives so openly, Moses implicitly poses questions that each of us must answer for ourselves, challenges us to engage in self-reflection and self-scrutiny, and reminds us that the world of the future is ours to mold and shape. He calls for us all to consider our role as potential super-champions—advocates for the arts committed to insuring their place in the future. He offers us a journey that is emblematic of what theatre for young audiences can be—a journey of self-discovery, a road of questions marked by questions that provoke new questions while resisting easy answers.

All in all, Moses sounds a clarion call for the right of our children to develop their full intellectual and physical potential, but their creative potential as well.

Let's heed the call. Happy reading.

Ben Cameron
Executive Director, Theatre Communications Group, 2005

PREFACE

It seems that I was destined for a career involving children. As a teenager, I worked with younger children in Boy Scouts and as a babysitter. I was a summer camp counselor for most of my late teen and college years. I started out in college as a chemistry major, but quickly realized that I did not want to work in a laboratory, so I switched to psychology, and went off to graduate school intending to become a child psychologist. In fact, I hold a master's degree in developmental psychology, which – as you may imagine – has always been useful to me in my theatrical life.

The theatre was always my "hobby." I had a reputation for making up stories as a child, and I loved to "act up" in front of a crowd. As a boy, I participated in children's theatre experiences, playing such challenging roles as a dwarf in *Snow White*, and—perhaps my signature role—the Cowardly Lion in *The Wizard of Oz*. In college, although a psychology major, I tried out for plays whenever I could, and was often cast, which put somewhat of a strain on my academic achievements.

If you are reading this, you have some interest in theatre yourself, so it will not come as a surprise to you that, while splitting my life between psychological research into human behavior and the art of creating imaginative and communicative theatrical behavior, the place where I felt more alive and happy and where most of my friends were found was in the theatre.

I knew I was going to be concerned with children, and helping them to reach their fullest potential as human beings. As an American male, I wanted to help American boys to be comfortable with their emotions, to become expressive and caring men. I wanted to help all young people grow up knowing the power of a story to inspire feelings and actions. I wanted young people to be whole creatures who could know the full range of what it might mean to be human.

Instead of devoting myself as a psychologist to *curing* children who had taken a wrong step in their emotional development, I switched fields, and decided to work on *keeping* healthy children healthy, by giving them the fullest possible exposure to the arts.

It has been over forty years since the day I made that career change, and I have had a chance to see the field of theatre for young audiences (TYA), and the related concept of children's drama, evolve in many powerful ways. This small collection of essays is an attempt to give some perspective to where I think we are, or should be, heading.

I have divided my thoughts into three areas: politics, artistic practice, and the practical management of the American TYA movement. The first section is constructed out of my own philosophical perceptions of society and its needs. I will try to create a logical argument to support a national policy for providing all of the arts for all young Americans. I am not so naïve as to assume that our nation's political leadership will actually do what I wish they would do to enable arts to flourish in our schools and communities, but I also know that nothing will happen at all if we don't have some vision of what we think should happen.

The second section is devoted to examining how I make theatre for young audiences, and why I do it that way. This is by no means a prescription for how you do it, or why, but it may be useful for you to have something to which to compare your own artistic vocation. I will be most happy if this section of the book produces a multitude of arguments as to why it should be done some other way entirely. But these techniques and rationales know the full range of what it might mean to be human.

Instead of devoting myself as a psychologist to *curing* children who had taken a wrong step in their emotional development, I switched fields, and decided to work on *keeping* healthy children healthy, by giving them the fullest possible exposure to the arts.

It has been over forty years since the day I made that career change, and I have had a chance to see the field of theatre for young audiences (TYA), and the related concept of children's drama, evolve in many powerful ways. This small collection of essays is an attempt to give some perspective to where I think we are, or should be, heading.

I have divided my thoughts into three areas: politics, artistic practice, and the practical management of the American TYA movement. The first section is constructed out of my own philosophical perceptions of society and its needs. I will try to create a logical argument to support a national policy for providing all of the arts for all young Americans. I am not so naïve as to assume that our nation's political leadership will actually do what I wish they would do to enable arts to flourish in our schools and communities, but I also know that nothing will happen at all if we don't have some vision of what we think should happen.

The second section is devoted to examining how I make theatre for young audiences, and why I do it that way. This is by no means a prescription for how you do it, or why, but it may be useful for you to have something to which to compare your own artistic vocation. I will be most happy if this section of the book produces a multitude of arguments as to why it should be done

PREFACE

some other way entirely. But these techniques and rationales worked for me, and seemed to reach the intended audiences.

The final section is really about what it meant to me to be a producing director for many, many years. How political theory and artistic intent can become actualized in the real world, when things like school bus schedules, and artists' egos have to be factored in to one's mission and budget plan. This part of the book is intended to let you know that things may not work out exactly the way you think they will, but that embracing the probability of reality interfering with your plans is much better than assuming that it won't.

This book would not exist at all if it were not for the hundreds of actors, playwrights, designers, educators, administrators, board members, donors, publishers, carpenters, seamstresses, prop artisans, musicians, dancers, ushers, house managers, bus drivers, custodians, and myriad of others who bought into one simple premise, that our children deserve our best efforts, and nothing less. I wanted to put great artists telling great stories into living contact with our children, and let the natural force of artistry do the rest. Those unnamed hundreds were the enablers. Many of them live in my memory as major contributors to the work of the past forty years, but to name them all would be impossible, and to name only a few of them would be a disservice to the others. They made it possible for me to see the joy and understanding on the faces of literally millions of children that have been touched, some of them in a permanent way, by the magic of the theatre. They also made it possible for me to evolve into what I have become, and to them all I can only say, "Thank you!"

— Moses Goldberg, 2005

THE POLITICS OF THEATRE FOR YOUNG AUDIENCES

THE POLITICS OF THEATRE FOR YOUNG AUDIENCES

1. CHILDHOOD, EDUCATION AND SOCIETY

A functional society's greatest asset is its children. Certainly, there have been human societies that were dedicated to some other goal—pure hedonism, or celibate religious fervor—and in which children were considered irrelevant. But for a society which wants to continue to have a future, a life span, as a society—children are the means for ensuring continuity.

It is therefore important to any such functional society to develop some means for the protection of children, and their nurturance and development to a point where they can become contributors to, and perpetuators of, that society. The human baby is born in a relatively helpless state. There must be some social structure in place to ensure that they receive basic necessities until they reach an age when they can provide for their own needs. In relatively primitive societies, that age might be as young as eleven or twelve. But as society has become increasingly sophisticated, the skills needed to survive and prosper have become correspondingly more sophisticated. In the industrialized portions of today's world, the child typically receives some level of protection, at least until the age of eighteen.

Generally, protections for the developing child can be divided into two major arenas: inside and outside of the family. Once again, there may be specific cultures where this distinction is blurred. In a traditional African tribal village there may truly exist a sense that the whole village is "family". But in modern American society there is a pretty clear separation between family influences on child development, and those provided by the larger society.

Inside the American family there exists a wide range of attitudes and practices. Families in our "salad bowl" culture descend from many cultural patterns, from many nationalities, many religious affiliations, many sub-cultures of economic and social status, and sub-sub-cultures based on parental interest or age or expectation, etc. For the first three or four years of life, the family is absolutely dominant in the shaping of a child's perceptions and values. Unless a child is an orphan, or removed from the family by a court order, these important early years are exclusively guided by the parents, siblings, or members of an extended family group. The principal result of this early influence is that the cultural patterns to which the child is exposed will tend to repeat themselves into this new generation. As might be expected, the child learns to imitate the language and customs of his family group. To give just one example, the children of Eastern European Jewish Republicans are likely to grow up with values and customs, even food preferences, that will be very different from the children of Hispanic Catholic Democrats. America is a land of diversity, and that is either our blessing or our curse. But as long as it remains true, the children growing up in American families will have diverse customs, values, and beliefs.

How our society will influence our children in matters outside of the family is strongly affected by the decisions we make on how to deal with that diversity. External society can make a basic choice to celebrate that diversity, or it can choose to regret it, and work to counteract it, in effect, to try to homogenize its future citizens. Many societies are not faced with this decision, as they are already homogenized. If every one in your village has the same ethnic background, the same religion, the same socioeconomic status, the same basic belief system, you can assume that your neighbor and you also have very similar values. But if you consider that the United States as a whole constitutes one large society, then clearly we have to find some way to allow different families to produce children with very different values. Finding a way to permit that diversity, and still build a strong society is our unique challenge in the modern world. Obviously, the arts have a significant role to play in meeting this challenge and elsewhere in this book that issue will be explored. But the first and most important tool society uses to shape its children, and prepare them to be functioning adults, is the loosely defined methodology called our education system.

Before we can examine how a society develops an education system, we must address a more basic issue: the question, of which version of a future society we are preparing for. Is the function of education to preserve the *current society*—the status quo; to educate young people to the same values that we educators hold, or that we taxpayers who pay for the education hold, and therefore, to perpetuate those institutions we adults of today find important? Or is the purpose of education to serve a different system, a *society of the future*, a society we don't even know about yet, a society that we adults don't know how to prepare for? If you make the decision that you're going to prepare young people for a society which doesn't even exist and that we don't even know about yet, then you are accepting a massive challenge. How can we prepare our children for a world that they will know but we will not? How can we train our young people to make decisions when we don't even know what the choices are going to be, or what the world they're going to face is going to look like? Then, if you factor in the diversity issue, all of these children (with all of the normal differences to be expected among normal individuals) are coming to the education system from different backgrounds, different ethnic groups, different religions, different economic expectations, different attitudes towards themselves and their neighbors, in short with very different values. It becomes a daunting task to design an education system that has even the slightest chance of working effectively.

How much easier it would be if we assumed that the goal for our education system is really to make everybody think alike, to have everyone learn exactly the same skills and/or values, to have everybody perpetuate today's society exactly as it is today. In the short term that sounds like a much more achievable goal—something we might actually accomplish. But that approach might also be short-sighted and might doom our society to stagnation and a descent into either decadence or deterioration. It is also an approach that may be rendered meaningless as conditions change in the environment.

One example, perhaps, will make the case: There was a time, not very long ago, in our society when women and men played very specific roles. Men went to work and earned a living. Women stayed home and raised children and cooked and cleaned. In most American cities there was an education system designed to maintain that social status. Girls took home economics classes in high school, and rarely went on to college, unless they were going to be teachers or nurses—the only professions that regularly welcomed women. Men took advanced math classes, or industrial shop classes, and knew they needed a good job if they were to be successful in society. The education system confidently prepared young people for the roles they were to play in society.

But in a relatively brief period of about twenty years, that society disappeared. Along came World War II when men had to go away to war, and women had to take on some of their critical jobs in the industrial workplace. Along came pills for birth control and family planning became an actual possibility. Jet travel and television and electric dishwashers and Civil Rights and a myriad of other changes also came along. And society was forced to change. A realignment of gender roles was only one of the tangible results.

Was this change anticipated by the brilliant educational minds of the 1930s and 40s? Did the system of public education make it possible for us to efficiently adapt to the changes? Did our schools teach women how to manage their expectations so that a career outside the home would become a part of their plan? Did men learn how to balance nurturing relationships with bread winning so that they could be good role models for their children? Can we make the claim that the educators of that period guided the children of that generation toward a better realization of their new roles in society? The basic answer to all of these questions is that they did not.

That is only one example; it would be easy to multiply other instances of changes to society that have come about in our own lifetimes. (Think of how well or how poorly educators prepared children in schools during the 1970s for the computers that they would all be using by the time they were parents themselves, as another example.) What are the educators of today doing to make it possible for the next generation of children to adapt to the changes that inevitably will face them after we are gone?

In the previous examples, educators were, for the most part, slow to adapt to the changing needs of an evolving social system, but sometimes educators are ahead of public change. After the Soviet Revolution in 1917, the new leaders of the U.S.S.R. determined that they had massive social changes to effect. They needed to change the serfs of old tsarist Russia and its client states into Communists with a strong political sensibility and a new sense of worker supremacy. Starting with the school systems, but also investing seriously in the role of the arts as a tool for reshaping social values, Lenin and his comrades succeeded in reshaping an entire culture in a matter of only a decade or so. Like the U.S., they were dealing with a wide range of cultures as they attempted to mold the fifteen separate Socialist Republics, and the dozens of ethnic tribes and language groups into a single Socialist state. In the 1990s, when the Socialist system collapsed for a variety of economic and social reasons, the educators were less prepared and their citizens, too, were suddenly faced with a society in a state of change for which there had been little or no educational preparation. It is too soon to know whether they will survive as a single society, fragment into dozens of smaller cultures again, or revert to some type of tsarist-like dictatorship. But the original plan, initiated back in the 1920s, was a bold one—to use the education system as a tool to reshape a society.

What can we, in modern America, do to insure that the next generations are ready for the changing world that will confront them? Instead of insisting on the equivalent of home economics or industrial shop classes, how can we shape our curriculum to open the doors to the future for our children? Is it possible to design such a curriculum and still nurture diversity in our multicultural society? The answers to these questions depend partly on the degree to which we, as a society, value our children and our future, but also on the degree to which we adults can tolerate the risk of having our own children mix with those from other cultures, or learn thought processes which might lead them to ask tough questions about the values of today.

If one were inclined to be pessimistic, one could point to evidence that we in contemporary American society value our children very poorly. In what esteem do we hold those who work with children? How well paid is the child care worker? To what extent are teachers honored, and how does their salary compare to a doctor's or a plumber's or a used car salesperson's? When the elected officials charged with planning our future continually raise the national debt ceiling—seemingly an annual event—how do they expect that our children will pay off all those trillions of dollars of debt? When the local school board decides that a good source of revenue might be the installation of candy and soda dispensers in our high schools, how do they imagine that our children will make the connection between snack time and a lifelong practice of healthy nutrition?

On the other hand, it is politically desirable to promote and protect children and the educational system, which is the principal way society affects children. We commit ourselves to health care for all children. Our society has banned cigarette advertising that might reach young people. We often increase funding for public education, although typically without applying any real knowledge as to how that money will be spent to effect changes. We are now talking about *accountability* in education, which really means that we want to measure what the child has learned. That doesn't guarantee that they are learning the things that will help them in the world of the future, but at least it does mean that we think we need to make sure that they have learned *something*. And slowly, very slowly, we have begun to increase teacher's salaries, and talk about teaching standards as a national goal.

The most encouraging sign is that it has once again become acceptable to talk about the child's *potential* as a concept, which was, perhaps, the fundamental idea in John Dewey's early philosophy of education—a progressive approach which many consider the foundation of our modern education system. If you want the child to evolve into an adult who is prepared for some unknown shift in the social spectrum, the best way to do that is not to set up some arbitrary benchmark of material that must be learned, but rather to set up a system that pushes every child toward his or her own highest potential. And that system should recognize that a certain child may have a very high potential in some sphere of knowledge or activity, and a relatively low potential in some other sphere. We should make it our business to broaden that child in every area in which that specific child can be broadened. For example, if a certain child has a physical ability, that child should be developed to reach his fullest potential as a moving physical being. Most genuine educators would agree that that is the basis behind our sports programs, not to find the person who can run the fastest and throw the discus the furthest, but to help each child develop to their physical best. In the same way, we should have the goal of developing each child to their best in each and every sphere of knowledge or ability. The mission should be to consider each child as a potential success at whatever they do best, not to assume that all children will be equally successful at all things.

Probably, the best way to achieve that mission is to empower the classroom teacher to a much higher degree. No educational system that puts the highest priority on goals that are mandated from above can factor in the child's individual needs or strengths and weaknesses. Only the classroom teacher is in a position to evaluate and recognize each child's potential, and to design an individualized program of instruction to allow that child to reach that potential. If our educational system is to succeed in the way that I am describing, the classroom teacher must become an educational designer and not—as they too often find themselves today—forced to act the role of a babysitter, a security guard, a record keeper, or an administrator of standardized tests. They must be trained and empowered to evaluate each child in their care, and design a program for that specific child to stretch his or her achievement until it reaches his or her own maximum potential.

Obviously, this approach is harder, and some may find it scary. How do you measure accountability when each child is working at a different pace and on a different objective? How can you prove that tax dollars are being spent wisely when no one yardstick can possibly measure all children the same way? There is such a measurement tool, and it is called the *portfolio*. It has appeared quite recently in several forward-thinking educational systems, and it is, perhaps oversimplified, a collection of each child's best work. Creating and developing a child's portfolio involves a personal interaction between the student and the educational designer, i.e., the teacher.

Each entry into the portfolio might represent a choice by the student. Each entry is also subject to continual revision and is, in a sense, never finished. It exists as one element in a body of work. Each element informs all of the other elements in the body of work, but each can also be seen as a stand-alone piece. The collection of pieces demonstrates the evolution of the child's skills over time, as more and more mature work is added. In all of these ways, and in more ways besides, the process of developing a portfolio is critically similar to the process of developing a work of art. In a subsequent essay I will discuss further the relevance of arts processes to the whole system of education. I introduce it here as a means of providing some accountability for the teacher whose objective is pushing each individual child toward a cluster of successes in a range of unique potentials, as opposed to reducing each child to a number on a standardized test.

I understand that the taxpayers will never be able to completely abandon the test score as a measure of a school's success and, in fact, Dewey considered a balance between the traditional learning of facts and the progressive focus on processes to be the most valid approach. But standardized test scores usually reflect learning that is relevant only to the content of the test. Teachers end up teaching the test's content, and while that may be beneficial to the extent that it is a good test—a test that has some relationship to knowledge or skills that can relate to real world needs of the individual—in those cases where the test is hyper-generalized and rewards memorization over thought process, that classroom time might be better used in teaching the child to find his or her own strengths and develop them.

Good teaching is much harder than most politicians think it is. In fact, good teaching is a very political act in that it is, in some small way, preparing society for its unknown but inevitable future. And since a functional society's greatest asset is its children, those individuals asked by society to protect and prepare that asset should be its most honored citizens.

2. ON A NATIONAL ARTS POLICY

Nations have policies toward all sorts of things, whether they define them specifically, or not. At one end of the spectrum, national policy can be spelled out in great detail. It can be enacted into a set of laws or statutes, it can be budgeted and funded, it can be debated publicly or in smoke-filled rooms, and it can even be the focus of an election year issue. At the other end of the spectrum, there are areas of concern that are never specifically codified into law or budgetary principle, but are still a well-rehearsed tendency, and a recognizable national trait. One can even create stereotypes based on perceived policies, which then can evolve into prejudices.

For example, imagine if you will that a certain nation has a policy toward the treatment of foreigners. It may be manifest in strict immigration laws, which may spell out how much or how little property a non-citizen may own, or whether they can ever be allowed to become a full-fledged citizen. There may be quotas that limit how many visas can be given to individuals from specific countries, or how many may obtain work permits, or own radio stations. Or this "policy" may never be codified as law, but simply be expressed as a national trait, welcoming or distancing strangers from our daily activities, enjoying a certain level of curiosity about visitors, or remaining completely aloof from them.

In such a variety of ways, nations have policies and/or attitudes toward arts and culture. Some have government agencies, (perhaps something called a Ministry of Culture) to monitor, regulate, or support cultural or artistic activities. Others have no formal code of laws, but have informal attitudes and customs which generally dictate how cultural or artistic activities are to be treated. Some link cultural activities to their formal system of education, others separate them completely. Some countries honor individual artists: in Japan a Noh performer, or in Indonesia a shadow puppet master, may be given a pension from the state and designated as a National Treasure. In England, a wonderful actor or painter may be knighted. In other countries, there is no recognition for the individual. In the U.S.A., for example, individual artists are prohibited from receiving direct funding from the federal government.

Many societies feel ambivalent about expressing support for the arts. Because they are intangible, because they can challenge moral boundaries, because they can encourage alternate realities, they can be perceived as a threat to a social structure trying to isolate or protect itself. There may also be a sense that supporting the arts requires a certain perspective, a certain maturity, as a nation.

This understanding is well-articulated in John Adams' famous quotation:

> I must study politics and war that my sons may have liberty to study mathematics and philosophy. My sons ought to study mathematics and philosophy, geography, natural history, naval architecture, navigation, commerce and agriculture in order to give their children a right to study painting, poetry, music, architecture, statuary, tapestry, and porcelain.

Adams suggests that at least three generations must pass before arts policy makes sense for a young nation, and indeed, cultural policies are often developed later in a society's life cycle, and may be articulated with some reservations. But hopefully, the arts command the attention and energy of large segments of society. They matter, and often to those in the society with leadership roles. Eventually, some statement of a national artistic policy should be articulated.

There are several international agencies that attempt to study and report on cultural policies as they compare in various parts of the world. CultureLink, for example, maintains a website (*www.culturelink.org*) which includes a searchable database of cultural policies for most of the European and many Asian nations. Canada is currently included in their database, although the U.S.A. is not.

Basic to any arts policy is a statement, again either explicit or implicit, as to the value of the arts, and the need for any nation to encourage their existence. Often, these justifications begin with the awareness that future generations will judge a society by its artifacts, especially its art works. We know a lot about the world

POLITICS: ON A NATIONAL ARTS POLICY

of Ancient Greece from its surviving architecture, its statues, its friezes, its plays. We have an understanding of Elizabethan England from our knowledge of the works of Shakespeare and other playwrights. The legacy we Americans leave will be interpreted by the scholars of the future who will study the works of art we create during our lifetimes. Our arts become our heritage, and give evidence of our lives and accomplishments.

But other ideas—arguments more meaningful to citizens here and now—can also be a part of the rationale for arts policy. For example, the arts document our differences. They enable us to understand each other by vicariously living through some vision or action that belongs to a subculture that we must live with, but never be a part of. A play about the black experience can provide black audiences with a sense of recognition and inclusion, but it can also provide white audiences with an empathic new understanding of their neighbors' reality.

The arts express our needs, our frustrations, our passions. They enable us to project strong emotions, and have those emotions witnessed by audiences. We cannot scream on the street without attracting negative reactions, but we can scream in a dance or in a painting and our pain becomes perfectly acceptable in a social setting.

And beyond just expressing ourselves, the arts also communicate. Isolated in our minds and bodies, we nevertheless yearn to be a part of a community, and have them truly know us. By creating art, we reveal ourselves to the universe. That same scream awakens compassion and understanding in others, who accept our passions (and maybe even us) a little bit better for having witnessed our playing out these strong emotions.

The arts can also act as a guide or commentary to our lives.

15

Through humor we can attempt to instruct our fellow creatures on the foolishness of their ways. Or we can debate social issues in a relatively safe environment, and show alternate ways of living to our peers. A play about fictional characters living through relevant social issues is a forum for the artist/playwright to admonish his listeners to be aware of their own foibles, or society's dangers.

The arts, especially the performing arts, can also bring us together. To be part of an orchestra or a theatre troupe requires that we work in unison with a group of others. Collaboration on a joint vision is a precious part of our need to be in harmony with our fellow creatures. To lose one's self in commitment to a group goal can be a gift, which is then multiplied by the number of participants, and received as a communal event by the viewers. The audience's shared existential moment, in which each individual member experiences a heightened understanding and empathy, and each of us is aware of our neighbors, who are having a very different experience, but all of these experiences are resulting from the communal act of being an audience, is one of the very few ways we Americans, with all of our many differences, can feel united.

These reasons can be multiplied: the arts give us self-confidence; they make us unique; they allow us to fantasize alternate realities; they give us joy. For all of these reasons, and many more besides, society ought to support and nurture opportunities for all citizens of all ages to participate in the arts as both creators and audience members.

Cultural policies, where they are articulated, often focus on several important criteria. Is the national policy intended to *dictate* the kind of art that will be supported, or is it intended to *encourage* a wide range of types of art? In some circumstances, society may find it necessary to *censor* or license works of art. Where art is encouraged, is the implementation *centralized*, controlled by a national board or committee, or is it *decentralized*, where control is implemented at regional or community centers? Does it take a position relative to the *traditional* art forms, or does it permit or promote new experimentation, and cutting-edge, even *avant-garde*, approaches? Does it reward a high level of artistry for an *elite* audience or a wide range of arts abilities for a *broad-based* audience? Does it go even further and address arts *participation* by large numbers of amateur artists? And normally, it must also address issues of *funding*. Does the government provide financial support (and under what conditions) for individual artists or arts agencies; does it provide financial incentives for private citizens or corporations to support the arts—perhaps by allowing tax write-offs for such contributions; or does it merely encourage private arts funding with no national policy of support?

In the United States, arts policy is monitored by an organization called Americans for the Arts, which was formed in 1996 by the merger of the National Assembly of Local Arts Agencies and the American Council for the Arts. As revealed on its website (*www.artsusa.org*), it has three primary goals:

- Increasing public and private sector support for the arts

- Ensuring that every American child has access to a high-quality arts education; and

- Strengthening communities through the arts.

These three goals are reflected in the mission statement of the National Endowment for the Arts (NEA), which is the U.S. governmental agency charged with the articulation and implementation of U.S. arts policy. As stated on its website (*www.*

arts.endow.gov), it is as follows:

> The National Endowment for the Arts enriches our Nation and its diverse cultural heritage by supporting works of artistic excellence, advancing learning in the arts, and strengthening the arts in communities throughout the country.

Both the official government agency and the citizen group that monitors them stress the same three goals: finding *support*, i.e. money for the arts; *learning* in the arts, especially by children; and the role of the arts in the life of the *community*.

Unfortunately, the NEA is given very few resources in our current national budget. The agency exists; it is able to formulate a statement of objectives; it has a small staff with which to implement its goals; and it has small amounts of money, which it uses to spotlight significant programs of high quality. By giving a few dollars to a few worthy projects, the NEA is at least able to illuminate "best practices" and great artistry. This token support hopefully acts as an imprimatur to encourage private philanthropy and public attention. The other national policy which impacts the arts is through our national income tax code, which allows deductions for donations to non-profit agencies that serve the public good. Although not specifically aimed at the arts, this policy benefits arts groups which can solicit funding and offer some tax incentive for donors. But the fiscal resources seem terribly inadequate for the noble statement of goals.

All three goals are important, and probably interdependent in a way that makes achieving one of them unlikely unless the other two are addressed. "Support" for the arts is money, of course, but also attention and advocacy. In a world where advertising exists on billboards, television, newspaper, even shoes and candy bars, how can focus be generated to highlight significant arts events? Sometimes such focus is created by an arts event being controversial—as the arts must be occasionally if they are to challenge our complacency and narrow world-view. And while one might deplore the negative publicity such an event creates, it may not be altogether a bad thing, because it also tends to draw out champions who will defend the sometimes controversial nature of art. Would our nation be well served if more actual dollars of support were directly appropriated for the arts? Since most of the money now available goes to give the stamp of approval to projects of national significance—"works of artistic excellence" as the mission statement reads—very little can be said to directly serve the community presence of the arts, or the exposure of learners, especially children. Ironically, the area where arts support might have the biggest impact – ensuring that all children are exposed to high quality art, has been seriously under-funded, and only recently has a little bit of extra arts money been funneled into this primary area. More can be done. Support for arts learning is directly examined in the next essay.

"Arts in the life of the community" is, of necessity, community defined, and I also devote a subsequent essay to the uniqueness of locally produced arts interchanges. Basically, the objective is to make the arts *visible* and *relevant*. In the tribal culture of long-ago and far away, the village storyteller may have been the repository of values; in his treasury of stories were contained the basic rules of social interaction. How can we make the arts agencies of today's complex and varied communities equally central to the social compact?

Most of my career and expertise has been focused on the middle goal "learning in the arts", as the NEA states it, or "access to a high-quality arts education" in the words of the Americans for the Arts. (The difference between the two statements, of course, is that the NEA's is broader, promoting lifelong learning, whereas the citizen group is focused on children.) In the first essay in this book, I proposed that children were critical to the survival and evolution of a functioning society. It therefore follows that a society which claims "arts learning" as a goal, and which also values its children, should be putting a high priority on making arts learning a part of each child's life while they are in the state-sponsored educational system, and beyond. While it is essential to have a national arts policy that is widely promulgated and receives sufficient resources, it is especially important to examine arts policy as it applies to the one area where society has an acknowledged role to play in preparing the society of the future —the educational system. Let us turn, therefore, to the basic way that arts penetrate, or ought to penetrate, the educational system.

3. THE THREE-LEGGED STOOL

In the first essay in this book, I have claimed that children are essential to a functional society, and in the second I have sought to point out the importance of a national arts policy that includes arts learning, especially for children. Let me now attempt to make the case for arts education that is funded by our educational systems.

If we agree that children should be exposed to the arts, in a democratic society like the U.S.A. those opportunities should be available to *all* children, not only the children of the wealthy, who might expose their own children to the arts as a perquisite belonging to the upper classes. The educational system reaches all children, albeit many through private or parochial schools. Most local educational systems, especially in the public sector, are limited in financial resources, to be sure, but the limitations facing arts funding in our society are even more intense. Arts are still considered frills in most governmental budgetary planning. The argument might be made that it is important to grant some token money to the arts so that our nation seems enlightened, and to show some concern for our place in posterity, but funding the arts at a high level is not really likely when we get down to discussing tax dollars. But everyone, even fiscal conservatives, understands that we must have a strong education system. *Our economy absolutely depends on a continual supply of well-trained workers, and future consumers with disposable income.* The schools must, therefore, continue to graduate young citizens with the skills to compete in a global marketplace and the wisdom to continue our nation's leadership role in an increasingly complex world. In today's political reality, a strong educational system is not negotiable.

How do the arts make the educational system stronger? What difference does it make if prospective employees or consumers have arts education in their background? Why should the schools — who increasingly must show accountability to the taxpayers —spend precious classroom time and money on something called art?

There have been many published research reports, and summaries of research reports which focus on the value of arts as a core area in a child's education. One such summary, with which I was peripherally involved several years ago, is *Building a Case for Arts Education: an Annotated Bibliography of Major Research*, a 1990 Monograph published by the Kentucky Alliance for Arts Education and the Kentucky Arts Council, and compiled by John McLaughlin. This document proposed an eleven-point, research-based, case statement for arts education highlighting currently acceptable education concerns, which I quote in its entirety:

1. The arts enhance students' creativity and increase creative thinking and problem-solving ability.

2. The arts are an integral part of human development in dimensions such as use of both hemispheres of the brain; development of cognitive, affective and psychomotor skills; and learning styles.

3. The arts increase communication skills vitally needed in today's complex society with its emphasis on technology and mass communication.

4. The arts enhance basic literacy skills (literacy here being defined more broadly than just fundamental reading skills) to include cultural literacy and literacy of non-verbal stimuli.

5. The arts enable students to acquire aesthetic judgment, a skill which enhances daily life and affects individual choices as well as group decisions concerning the human environment.

6. The arts develop self-esteem and help students gain a more positive self-concept. Low self-esteem is considered the root of major societal problems such as violence, teenage suicide, and substance abuse.

7. The arts provide students better cross-cultural understanding through knowledge of civilizations and cultures past and present. Cross-cultural understanding is significant in terms of the international nature of the economy. In terms of human relationships, failure to understand the pluralistic nature of society often leads to racial and ethnic tensions.

8. The arts improve the school atmosphere and can aid in improving student attendance and decreasing the dropout rate.

9. The arts provide numerous career opportunities both in the commercial/entertainment industry and in the not-for-profit sector.

10. The arts improve student performance in other subject areas.

11. The arts are a valuable teaching tool in working with special populations such as students with mental or physical handicaps, those with limited English proficiency, or the economically disadvantaged.

These eleven areas of concern are central to the goals of the school system, and apply whether one chooses to focus education on today's values and preserving the *status quo*, or whether, as I discussed in a previous essay, one chooses to prepare young people for an unknown future world by promoting individualized instruction which pursues the goal of each child reaching his or her fullest potential.

As I have seen them practiced in educational settings, theatre and drama provide students with additional *aesthetic, pedagogical,* and *psychological* values. Aesthetically, theatre and drama are *enjoyable*, and they allow for *expression, participation, empathy* and *identification* with others, and a possible purging of negative or disturbing emotions. Pedagogically, they present the child with a *content* area (the subject of the play or scene); *conventions* (styles of theatrical presentation, rules for understanding the art of theatre); *cultural learning* (other lives, other cultural patterns); and a chance to fully consider *ethics* (all drama involves conflict, and the most prevalent conflict is the one between good and evil). Psychologically, the drama brings socialization skills, and a chance for personal growth and *maturation*, as the child works through problems vicariously, and then internalizes those aspects of the problem-solving that are most relevant to his or her current psychological or social needs.

When considered in this light, the arts are anything but a frill. All of these values are critical ones for the schools' mission, and many of them can be approached through the arts much more directly than through any other field or subject area. (And I do not even bring into the discussion those children—a small but very real percentage of the total—for whom the arts may represent the only way of reaching them and inspiring them to learn.) And research continues to support these claims for the arts. Scores on national standardized tests are almost invariably higher for students with exposure to the arts, and although most of the existing studies are limited in outlook and application, the sheer number of them and consistency of their positive results are beginning to penetrate the awareness of educational planners. When the Commonwealth of Kentucky completely revised its educational system in the early 1990s, the arts were actually included as a tested area, worth 7% of a school district's final grade, which determined whether that district was meeting its officially approved objectives. (Perhaps it should have been 20% or 70%, but one has to start somewhere.)

The Americans for the Arts maintains a website that lists current research supporting the arts (*http://www.americansforthearts.org/public_awareness*). To give only a few examples from the extensive list of documented results posted as I write this:

> Elementary students who attended schools in which the arts were integrated with classroom curriculum outperformed their peers in math who did not have an arts-integrated curriculum.

> Schools in South Carolina that made room in their schedules for the arts at the expense of other academic disciplines did not suffer a decline in standardized test

scores in the courses that lost time in the school schedule through the addition of the arts.

Sixth grade students who attended schools in which the arts were integrated with classroom curriculum outperformed their peers in reading who did not have an arts-integrated curriculum.

Troubled students involved in after school arts programs excelled in academics and school life beyond less troubled students in a national sample.

Regular, frequent instruction in drama and sign language created higher scores in language development for Head Start students than for a control group not offered drama and sign language.

Preschoolers who were given music keyboard lessons improved their spatial-temporal reasoning.

Much of the evidence for the effectiveness of the arts is relatively new. And budgetary pressures are still real in most educational systems. In order to implement arts in the schools, educators need a clear understanding of *how* the arts can be implemented. If, magically, there would be a general acceptance of the role the arts can play in helping children reach their fullest potential, and simultaneously a commitment to use the arts in the schools, there is still little understanding of *what* precisely needs to be done. If a school district made the decision to fully integrate arts as a core area in the curriculum, how exactly would they do it? Who would be responsible? How much would it—should it—cost?

One of the earliest comprehensive statements of what needs to happen in the arts to make them a full component of a child's education was the publication in 1977 of *Coming to our Senses: the Significance of the Arts for American Education*, by the Arts, Education and Americans Panel, (David Rockefeller, Jr.,

Chairman). This report makes many assertions about the value of the arts in accomplishing the overall mission of the educational system, which strongly parallel John McLaughlin's case statement quoted above. But it also goes on to spell out a three-pronged approach to arts education, and introduces the argument for making all three components essential and interdependent if the results are to be demonstrable and effective. The three ingredients in their recommendations for an effective arts program are: *arts instruction*, *arts processes incorporated into the classroom*, and *arts experiences*. To me, these three areas act as a three-legged stool, providing a solid foundation in the arts, maximizing the chances of influencing the child's total education, and significantly improving the chances of that individual child reaching his or her fullest potential as a human being and contributor to society.

Arts instruction involves all students learning the basic components of the major art forms, and having some experience at expressing themselves though that art form. In the area of theatre and drama, for example, it would include a basic vocabulary: understanding plot, character, theme, conflict, etc., and identifying them in works of art they make or see. It would include an opportunity for arts production: to move creatively, to physicalize a character, to invent dialogue through improvisation, to perform a rehearsed play before an audience of peers, etc. It should also include arts appreciation, whereby the participants can recognize the different media or genres in any one art form, the different contributions made, for example, by a director, playwright, actor, or designer; or the difference between Realism and Expressionism. Arts instruction should be offered in dance, music, theatre, and visual art. It should be offered to all children in elementary and middle schools and be available to high school students as well, with those students showing proficiency able to take advanced instruction as an elective. It should be offered by trained arts specialists, who are attached to and able to contribute in other ways to the life of the school communities. As specialists are considered vital to the school system in speech therapy, remedial reading, or physical education, arts specialists should be a regular part of a district's budget. Arts Education should be a recognized degree specialization in teacher training programs, which should, of course, be coordinating their preparation for certification with subject matter areas in their respective colleges. A seminal guidebook, *National Standards for Arts Education*, was published in 1994 by a Consortium of Arts Education Associations, and spells out specific skills and standards for evaluating arts learning at various levels of educational maturity. *Arts instruction* gives each child the opportunity to express themselves as a developing artist and to recognize and appreciate the artistic expression of others.

Arts processes as a part of the regular classroom environment refers to the way classroom teachers teach all of the other subjects covered in the school curriculum. It asks the classroom teacher to understand and utilize the mental processes integral to the arts as part of all of their classroom management and instruction. Artists think and process information in ways that are sometimes different from non-artists. They are more likely to associate ideas in non-logical ways. They frequently approach information using other abilities than strictly cognitive ones, and often with a "multiple intelligences" approach. They are not concerned as much with finding one right answer to questions as they are with finding multiple ways to express an idea. They are comfortable collaborating on the creation of a project. They are used to the idea of revising their creative work, perhaps never putting it into a "finished" state. They are relatively comfortable with the concept of criticism—especially when that critic is responding in a sincere way to how the art product makes them feel or think. A performing artist grows to accept the idea that the critic may be criticizing the artist's own voice, body, or imagination since those are the primary materials the artist brings to the interpretation of a play or musical score. For the artist, facts are less important than truths. *The goal of the classroom use of arts processes should be to make every teacher more flexible in how they teach*; willing to encourage students' use of multiple intelligences; willing to encourage open-ended and even fanciful thoughts; willing to allow for collaboration and the revision of work, especially in a portfolio assignment. Basically, this is just good, creative teaching that recognizes individual differences in learning styles, and balances the need to learn facts with the need to learn truths. Supporting this kind of teaching, for example, is the well known Project Zero at Harvard University which has become a nationally recognized influence on modern education reform. Their mission, from their website (*http://pzweb.harvard.edu*), is as follows: "… to understand and enhance learning, thinking, and creativity in the arts, as well as humanistic and scientific disciplines, at the individual and institutional levels." This component must be done by the regular classroom or subject area teacher, and it must therefore be an accepted part of teacher preparation in college education departments. The cost of this component is really zero, since it doesn't require any additional time or money, just a truly broadened approach to teacher training.

Regular use of arts processes by classroom teachers may also be seen to lead to the integration of arts content areas as teachers begin to understand how theatre processes, for example, can be used in the classroom to help students understand social studies, or music processes can relate to mathematics. And this may even lead to direct coordination of arts instruction with the classroom curriculum, as arts specialists and classroom teachers work together on these integrated units.

Arts experiences implies that all students will have the opportunity to come into contact with high quality, age appropriate works of art, often utilizing community resources beyond the actual school system. When the students actually get to experience a great performance of a play, or see up close an impressive oil painting, they receive many gifts: the joy of experiencing a great work of art, a chance to analyze its components by applying the arts appreciation they are learning, the inspiration to continue in their own artistic creations, a model of what can be achieved in that art form, a chance to share an arts experience with their classmates and teachers, an awareness that the community that they live in values them as arts learners and therefore provides these experiences for their enjoyment and growth, and many other benefits. Key to the success of this component is the quality of the arts experience. Going to a bad play or concert has the opposite of the desired result, since it may teach the students that the arts are boring. Age appropriateness is also important, and will be discussed at great length in a subsequent section of this book. The child should find the arts experience challenging and rewarding, neither so far beneath his or her interest that it becomes condescending, nor so far above that it becomes confusing. Funding may be more difficult to find for this component, as it acknowledges that the school system is reliant on the outside community for enrichment and completion of certain educational objectives. Field trip or enrichment money should be included in district budgets on a per child basis. Recognizing that wealthy schools will secure these kinds of experiences for their children through PTA donations, or family funding of field trips, districts and state governments should work to ensure that no child is left out of these experiences by providing them from public funds. These experiences should be provided by those elements of the community that have the interest and ability to do so—ideally the best professional arts agencies. These may be touring companies that come to the schools or performing groups or galleries that invite the children to come to them on field trips. Obviously, appropriate pre- and post-exposure activities should be carefully designed with the classroom teacher and the arts specialist as full collaborators. The passion and enthusiasm that can result from an exposure to the right *arts experiences* acts to justify and complement the work of the arts specialists, and the artistic thought processes used in the classroom.

In the real world, with all the many forces that act to limit budgets, or teacher preparation time, the inclusion of these three interdependent components will probably depend on the presence of champions, who will advocate and lobby for their everyday presence in the life of the school child. Probably, each of the three components will need its own champions to advocate and oversee their availability.

Arts instruction has built-in champions, the arts specialists. The relatively well established music and visual arts specialists have, respectively, strong national professional associations. They work singly and as a national voice to push for the inclusion of arts instruction in every child's life. Theatre and dance are much less visible, and many states do not have these as certified specialties. Dance instruction may be championed by versatile physical education specialists, and theatre often comes under the umbrella of an English teacher with a keen interest, although often this does not translate to the elementary school level, where creative dramatic activities would be most appropriate. The National Alliance for Arts Education was founded with the strong leadership of arts specialists, and the *Standards* document referred to above came out of their efforts. Hopefully, the mounting evidence for the positive impact of arts on educational achievement will win additional champions to this area.

Arts processes as a part of every classroom teacher's methodology needs to be championed by teacher educators in colleges of education. Whether they recognize it as arts based, or merely think of it as "multiple intelligences" or "differences in learning styles," teacher educators should be pushing pre-service teachers to focus on children's varying potential as learners, and on the use of different classroom strategies. Ideally, some direct instruction in the arts will also take place, possibly from an integrated course in arts methodologies, where not only can arts instruction be introduced, but arts processes can be shown to be relevant to other content areas. Once again, as research evidence mounts for the effectiveness of this approach, teacher training programs should be eager to embrace this dynamic and successful methodology.

Arts experiences must be championed by those able to provide the experiences. Some communities are fortunate to have top quality arts agencies with a total commitment to providing arts experiences for school age populations. These may be agencies with a broad mission to serve the entire community, or specialist agencies that focus only on school age populations. (This is the area with which I have been most closely associated throughout my own career, and it will be more fully explored in subsequent essays.) In other cities, the arts agencies provide those services reluctantly, only when they can get a special grant to do so, or not at all. Artists and community leaders who believe that every community should have strong local arts agencies need to recognize that the focus on students will have a long-term positive effect on developing widespread support for those arts agencies, as well as having the immediate effect of stimulating today's young audiences. There must also be a commitment, of course, from the school community to make full use of these resources, when they are available. This can come from the individual classroom teacher who values a field trip to a play or concert for the many benefits it will provide to the students, or it can come from a building principal or even a district superintendent who decrees a range of arts experiences for all the students under his or her jurisdiction.

The best solution of all, of course, would be to have super-champions—a few well-placed and farsighted individuals who are convinced of the value of the arts, and who make sure that all three components of arts education are available for all of the children under their influence. This can be a great educator, or a great political leader. Whatever the results of his political and social policies may have been, the fact the Vladimir Lenin saw the arts as useful to his long-term purposes made it very easy for the arts to be made available for almost every child in the newly formed U.S.S.R. Much of our early success at Stage One in Louisville came about because arts agencies, arts specialists, and classroom teachers interested in the arts were united by the vision of a school administrator – Jean Green, who served as Cultural Coordinator for the public schools at the time. During the late 1970's and early 1980's she made sure that all three components were present in most of the schools, and that the advocates for any one of the stool's legs were in close communication with the advocates for the other two legs. When the time comes, hopefully not too far distant, that a significant percentage of educational leaders like Jean Green in large and small school districts, and political leaders at all levels of US government, are themselves products of a school system where the arts were fully integrated into instruction, and where arts experiences represent cherished memories from their own school days, then a well-rounded arts program that uses all three components will be much easier to achieve for all children.

4. THE 100% AUDIENCE

In the United States, we tend to think of the living theatre as an art form enjoyed by a relatively elite segment of the population. The Broadway theatre is fairly expensive for a night's entertainment, particularly when you add in parking and dinner. People go to a Broadway "show" when they are on business expense accounts, or when they are on vacation in New York and looking for something special to do. Away from New York, there is a Broadway series in most major cities, where—for a fairly high ticket price—one can see touring musical shows with huge casts and excellent production values. The audiences at these performances tend to come from the affluent sectors of the community, although you will also find passionate theatre fans saving up for a special night at a well-loved show, perhaps one from which they have memorized the lyrics, having downloaded the original cast recording.

Slightly less expensive are the regional not-for-profit theatres, also found in most large cities. Here one often sees students, and less affluent theatre *aficionados*, or the occasional church group on a special excursion, but the core audience is drawn from the well-educated, upper income families, or those who choose to be perceived as playing a leadership role in the community. It is an indicator of civic recognition to serve on the board of such a theatre, or to be listed as a contributor on the donor page in the program. The largest cities have additional, smaller theatres, which tend to define themselves by their audience segment—there are *avant-garde* theatres that attract political liberals and social critics; there are dinner theatres that attract people celebrating special occasions; there are ethnic theatres that chiefly attract their respective minorities; there are gay theatres; and playwright's theatres; and theatres of and for a myriad of special needs. There are also college and university theatres that attract theatre majors, faculty members, and undergraduates who need to write play reports for class credit.

There is one type of theatre, however, that plays to nearly 100% of the potential audience. That is a theatre for young audiences (TYA) that plays during school hours—whether on tour to school assembly programs, or in their home theatre for school groups on field trips. (TYA performances done for public audiences as weekend matinees, or evening shows, draw audiences primarily from the same families that support the regional and Broadway theatres. There is much debate over the benefits and challenges of choosing to serve such an audience. Certainly, a TYA that performs for the public is programming and marketing very differently from one that chooses to play to school time audiences, and I devote an entire essay to this debate later in this volume.) But those TYA companies that choose to perform during school hours are doing plays developed and marketed for school children, and *nearly every child goes to school*—even the home schooled and those with manageable disabilities. Because the potential audience is virtually everyone of a certain age that lives in the community to be served, a different mindset must apply to the artists who presume to provide these theatrical experiences for such an inclusive audience.

There are increased opportunities when playing to the 100% audience but, as a trade off, there are increased responsibilities. Where the artist in an avant-garde theatre is free to challenge, or even shock the audience, there may be limits in the school based TYA. While spectacle is appropriate on the Broadway stage, and while young people also enjoy spectacle, there may be a need to justify visual delights with some redeeming social or instructional purpose. *Fundamentally, the TYA artist who plays for schools must understand the importance of finding the balance between art and education in all the work that is presented.* Because the performance takes place during school hours, it is essential that there be a willingness to negotiate in good faith with the objectives of the school system. Teachers and principals who commit time and money to bringing the performance to the children in their charge need to feel that the artists support their mission, and that the artists will also show sensitivity to the public nature of the school curriculum, where any parent or journalist can feel free to question or complain about any content to which the child may be exposed.

Perhaps the fundamental adjustment that the artist must make when programming for school children is the need to understand that the child does not make the choice to come to the theatre. The choice to attend is made by a school administrator or a teacher, and this person is selecting a program that a) they can justify in terms of its relationship to the school's curriculum—broadly defined; and b) that will be appropriate to the maturity and values of each and every one of the widely diverse students in their classes. Given that teachers are ultimately held accountable for the success of their students on standardized tests, how does going to this play help prepare them for the test? Given that the school day is crammed full of demands, both imposed from above, and keenly felt from within the classroom, how does going to this play move us forward to our goals? Within a single class one can find the children of devout and irreligious parents, politically conservative or liberal voters, hands-on and *laissez-faire* parenting styles, etc. The teacher needs to be certain that voluntarily taking the children on this field trip to the theatre is going to result in positive reactions from the parents, as well, of course, as a fun experience for the kids.

The theatre must do two things to help the teacher. It must provide information about how the play connects to the curriculum and it must provide any alerts as to sensitive material so that an informed choice can be made.

In many states, there exist published and approved educational objectives. These objectives include subject matter to be taught, but also dispositions and values which the school is responsible for passing on – such as "understanding diversity" or "working cooperatively". In Kentucky, for example, the current objectives were originally published as *TRANSFORMATIONS: Kentucky's Curriculum Framework* in 1993. Objectives are listed with numbers assigned to each, so that a theatre could include specific numeric references in all of their promotional literature. From among the dozens of objectives, here are a few which easily relate to almost any theatre performance:

> 1.3 Students construct meaning from messages communicated in a variety of ways for a variety of purposes through observing.

> 2.21 Students observe, analyze, and interpret human behaviors to acquire a better understanding of self, others, and human relationships.

> 2.24 Students appreciate creativity and values of the arts and the humanities.

> 5.4 Students use a decision-making process to make informed decisions among options.

Many others can also be shown to be relevant to one or more types of plays. Referencing these numbered goals, teachers can instantly justify a theatre experience for their students by pointing to the required code of objectives.

In addition, the plays' themes can be broadly identified for the teacher considering attending: "This play is about the early life of Benjamin Franklin;" or "This play is about the life cycle as found in nature." These specifics also allow the teacher to make a persuasive argument for bringing the class to the play. "It will help us in our unit on the American Revolution, by bringing the characters to life." "It will help inform our science project on life cycles." More obviously, the play may also be based on a book or story that the class is actually reading. If a group of students is studying *The Diary of Anne Frank* or *Tom Sawyer*, a performance of a play based on the book is easily dovetailed with the curriculum.

Sensitivity to possible controversy is also essential. Obviously, any use of mature language or subject matter must be disclosed, so that the teacher can let parents opt out of sending a child along, if necessary. In some religious faiths, plays about mysticism or the supernatural will upset parents, and their children should not be taken to such plays without careful preparation of both parent and child. In older classes, especially in middle or high school, where plays may deal with themes like suicide or sexuality, it is always better to disclose full information, even allowing apprehensive parents to read advance copies of scripts. It serves no benefit to the theatre if teachers are held hostage by administrators or parents because they exposed the children to controversial material. Of course, there are many classrooms where teachers can make excellent use of such edgy material—carefully preparing the students and their families, bringing home points made effectively in the play, and building classroom discussions or writing projects on the students' diverse responses to the play.

These two restrictions might lead the theatre artist to the conclusion that serving a school audience is packed with dangers.

If plays have to be chosen that relate to the curriculum, and cannot contain much that is controversial, why bother to serve such an audience? The answer should be obvious: it gives you the chance to reach *all* of the children. Every child should have a chance to experience high quality live theatre. Every child can and will be affected deeply by the empathy and identification that only caring about believable characters in threatening situations can provide. This is a unique opportunity to open up a child who might otherwise never have such a contact to the very powerful and very real magic of the theatre.

Besides, the restrictions raised are not really such onerous ones. Plays done for schools must have curriculum connections, but a play that had no learning potential would be of very little value anyway. The curriculum objectives, as published, are so broad, covering a myriad of subject areas—the whole range of human behavior, the mores of our society, and a chance to learn about other societies—that it is hard to imagine a play that cannot be made to sound relevant with a little examination, and some familiarity with the schools' objectives. A cynical observer might conclude that any play can be made relevant to the curriculum, and that an exploitive artist might justify anything that he or she wanted to do. (The same cynic might conclude that all teachers care about is high test scores.) While there is possibly a grain of truth in both assertions, the point is that as there is a payoff on test results from good teaching, there is also learning content in all good art. One does not have to compromise on artistry to find appropriate material for school-time audiences.

Addressing the second concern, I suggest that a play that contains noticeably controversial points is going to pull the children away from their suspension of disbelief so quickly, and with such a pervasive effect, that the play's purpose will be completely defeated. One profane or suggestive word, that is not perfectly sustained by the moment onstage, will elicit gasps or hoots from a middle school audience, and ten minutes may go by before they again attend to the necessary business of the play. Remember that an audience of school children, all pretty much the same age, with no parents or siblings watching, with their friends sitting next to them, and only a handful of teachers or chaperons in the theatre, are going to respond in an almost totally homogeneous way to anything onstage. The distraction of a forbidden topic or a nasty word—unless it is totally embedded in an honest reaction of a character they care about—will remind them that this is a forbidden subject, and pull them right out of the play. On those rare occasions when the play is so convincing that they do not notice that a school-time taboo has been broken, it is still possible that the teachers will notice the offense, and resent the fact that the theatre took the risk of embarrassing them in front of their students. It is probably best, during school-time performances, to honor both curriculum connections and teachers' sensitivity to controversy.

However, there is one very important school goal that the theatre must NOT embrace. *While I strongly advocate the blending of educational and aesthetic goals in these performances, education must never be allowed to dominate; must never even be allowed to seem to be the intended objective.* The arts can serve the education process in many ways, but only if they continue to be the arts. The theatre is not a piece of chalk, a tool designed to help teachers do their job. The theatre is a magical, perhaps spiritual, place where the audience can lose themselves in an empathic relationship with a character that leads them to transcend their own day-to-day existence. It can be uplifting and life-affirming. It can make us laugh or cry. It can change us both emotionally and intellectually. It can show us spectacle, or inspire us to imagine. It can never do these things if we are constantly aware that the theatre has an educational mission. I have always loved Federal Theatre pioneer Yasha Frank's quotation, "Children love to learn, but they hate to be taught." That seems to summarize my concern perfectly. We accomplish so much in the theatre precisely because the theatre does not seem to be teaching, and at that moment, it is teaching most effectively.

It should be the teacher's role, after the performance is over, to lead the students to analyze the production, to relate it to learning goals from the classroom, to apply it consciously to the curriculum. The artist should resist being drawn into that process. Even in after-play discussions, it should not be the job of the actor or other artist to say what the play "meant." "What do you think it meant?" is the only correct response to such a post-performance question. An actor may reveal his character's subtext—if a clever student is asking for it in a talk-back session—but never what it might mean to the particular student. That might suggest that we artists had a motive in presenting the play other than the only viable motive: to share an aesthetic experience. The theatre can be both educational and artistic, but only if it is artistic first and educational upon later reflection or after it is pointed out by someone other than the artist.

Many years ago there was a social movement to make effective use of television as a teaching tool. There was, and still is, concern that children spend many hours watching T.V., and most of it is not uplifting or informative. A drive was begun to create programming for young viewers that would be "educational." The best achievement to come out of that movement was the Children's Television Workshop's creation of *SESAME STREET*. This program has successfully taught the alphabet, and pronouns, and social concepts to generations of children. It has done so by never seeming to be educational. Every lesson is contained in a short dramatic scene, always built around a conflict—which is the essence of the dramatic art. There are a collection of well-known characters, each of whom has a role to play in working through the conflicts of the neighborhood, and the viewers quickly understand that each of them has a unique personality. Whether they are live actors or puppets, there is a relationship that is consistent, but that can still be surprising as they confront each other over small details. And in the process of laughing at them, or worrying about their petty problems, *we learn*. It is also worth noting that this is a program aimed at a 100% audience—all children can watch it, enjoy it, and learn because of it.

Theatre can serve a similar role for all children if it can reach them during school hours. As long as the entertainment and aesthetic purpose of theatre is never compromised, as long as the students are being delighted and are being led to care about characters with problems, and empathize as they solve those problems or learn to deal with them, then the theatre is also accomplishing major educational goals, and it can do so effectively for nearly all children, if it reaches them through the schools.

I have always believed that the theatre could and should be a populist art form. Since the basic content of theatre is human behavior, it is easily accessible to all. The vast film and television audiences are primed to enjoy the theatre, and it only requires a willingness to join in a communal experience of the art form as a live event to make everyone a theatregoer; that and a willingness by the artist to address his or her message to a larger audience. By incorporating the very proper concerns of the schools, we can reach all of the children, and by providing them with good theatrical experiences that entertain, primarily, and develop the audience, as a secondary phenomenon, we are also creating an audience of adults who might express a lifelong love of theatre.

5. ALL POLITICS IS LOCAL

The statement that "All politics is local," is attributed to Thomas P. (Tip) O'Neill, Jr., Democrat, Congressman from Massachusetts, and longtime Speaker of the House of Representatives (1977– 1987). Although O'Neill was regarded as one of the most visible leaders of our nation, an elected official for fifty years, and, as Speaker, third in line for the presidency, he claimed that his decision-making processes were always influenced by the comments and attitudes of his immediate constituency in North Cambridge. Required by his position to act globally, he never lost the habit of thinking locally, of making sure that his positions could be translated back home to the folks who elected him.

In a parallel way, the job description of an artist, particularly as a leader of a theatre company for young audiences (TYA), may be to *think globally, and act locally.* I like to think that the artistic director of a TYA Company plays a role similar to the village storyteller in a tribal society. The artistic director perpetuates the cultural literacy of the next generation, keeps alive the value system of the tribe, and teaches audiences how to apply history and ethics to decision making. In order to do that most effectively, he or she must have a global sense of right and wrong, a fundamental system of beliefs that he or she is passionate to share. But one must also know the audience; know their immediate history and customs. It is not enough to have a big idea; one must also know how to convey that idea to the young people in the present space and time.

And one must also understand the rules for doing business in the immediate environment of the theatre. All communities operate differently. The political and financial leaders of every

POLITICS: ALL POLITICS IS LOCAL

community may have similar goals, and may talk about the same values, but there is always a unique local way of making decisions, or distributing resources, or recognizing success or punishing failure. Perhaps this is simply a result of the varying personalities of the people in charge, but it is also very evident that different social customs evolve among different groups of people. In different parts of our huge nation, people don't even speak exactly the same language, although fifty years of television have smoothed out some of the differences. If one were to call a can of Coca-Cola a can of "pop," when the locals know it as a "soda" or a "coke," one would, however subtly, be branded as an outsider. A "doughnut" is a "cruller" in some regions, and regional differences in pronunciation are frequently the fodder for jokes on national television programs. There are also differences in ethnic makeup and diversity, percentages of people who follow different religions, divisions between liberals and conservatives, attitudes towards gambling and alcohol consumption, and many other regional differences. Loyalty to a particular sports franchise is another passion that separates us, one from another, even in cities that might only be a few miles apart.

The recognition of these regional variances is, perhaps, a principal reason that local control of school systems is one of the most ingrained features of American politics. All communities have local school boards, and those boards make the critical decisions as to curriculum, textbooks, personnel, calendars, facilities, etc. Educational mandates coming down from a federal or even from a state level are regarded with suspicion and mistrust. When they come attached to funds for implementation, they are usually followed—albeit with regional variances. When they come unfunded, they provoke even stronger antagonism.

Because of the latitude given to local educators, two elementary

43

school buildings only one mile apart can have vastly different environments and can turn out students with vastly different skills. For example, one can walk into a particular school building and instantly sense an atmosphere of creativity and individual worth—one can tell from the range of unique art works attached to the walls. In such a school building, students are not afraid to express emotions, even, under control, negative ones. (In fact, I believe that allowing negative emotions is the only way to teach the control necessary to manage them in society. What is forbidden can never be trained.) In the adjoining neighborhood, the school building might seem sterile and rigidly conformist. "Cookie-cutter" art work—or none at all—is on those walls. Students are rewarded for lining up straight and remaining orderly, whereas in the former school they earn praise for original thinking and enthusiasm for the learning process.

The same kinds of differences can be described in a business environment, or in a donor community, or in a gathering of artists. Some communities mistrust artists; it is almost impossible for them to qualify for a mortgage loan if they list "actor" as their occupation. In other places, ordinary business people are proud of the artists who call their community "home." Ask a taxi driver or a restaurant server if they know about the local theatre scene. They may not have complete and accurate performances schedules, but the pride of ownership in their voices will reveal the kind of attitude that locals have toward their very own arts groups. I have always been impressed with the community of Louisville, Kentucky, where I made my aesthetic home for twenty-five years (1978–2003). Louisville has a United Arts Fund, and ordinary people contribute money. In fact, thousands of people, *who never attend the arts themselves,* give payroll deductions and other gifts so that their children will have access to concerts, dance programs, and plays. In Louisville, and in a few other cities, one quickly gets the sense that "we do the arts here." This should make the job of "village storyteller" easier to do, but one must still understand the values of the specific community. One must appreciate that the leaders of the community have certain themes they want to make sure their children understand, and others to which they would prefer not to expose them. The artist, especially if he or she grew up in some different place, must have a way to make contact with this value system, and usually that happens by relying on the counsel of selected spokesmen for the community.

In most professional theatre companies, there is a specific division of leadership roles, which also acts to further underscore individual differences between arts agencies. Typically, theatres are led by a triumvirate: an artistic director, a managing director, and a board of trustees or directors. The titles may vary, and the particular individuals may even overlap, but the three functions generally follow a consistent pattern. The Artistic Director represents the aesthetic taste of the company. This person chooses the plays, hires the artists, and oversees the quality and standards of the performances. The Board represents the will of the community. They are the legal entity which operates the theatre, usually as a not-for-profit, tax-sheltered operation. They hire the artistic and managing directors, which implies that—by who they hire—they have the last word in defining aesthetic taste; and they approve all budgets, ideally raising much of the contributed support that enables the productions to go forward. The Manager acts, typically, as a liaison between these other two leaders, but also is charged with the business operations of the theatre – marketing, facility management, fiscal administration, etc. Generally, the manager's loyalty is to the position of artistic director, and, ideally, he or she will share that individual's defined taste.

The composition of the Board is a key element in making the

theatre a unique operation, focused on the needs of that particular community because the board is drawn from that particular community. Board members must be willing to speak up when seasons are being debated, and make sure that the professional staff understands the particular customs of the community. But the individual vision of the artistic director is an even more critical source of uniqueness, because that individual's talents and sensibilities will be their own, and no two artistic leaders will share exactly the same tastes and preferences. The artistic director's personal taste is the aesthetic wellspring of the theatre; he or she is expected to prefer his or her own judgment to that of all others. Obviously, this creates the possibility that the artistic director will be perceived as egoistic but, in fact, it is central to the job to have a strong sense of taste, and unshakable confidence in his or her own choices. By hiring and supporting that individual, boards and managers accept that distinctive artistic taste as completely appropriate for their environment.

Two things, therefore, operate to ensure that all theatres will be unique. One is the differences in composition of the communities they serve; the other is the particular tastes of their artistic leader. Consultants, or other experts, attempting to offer advice as to the strategies that might help that theatre reach its goals who do not consider these two defining sources will fail, as generic solutions do not work well in combating unique problems. But uniqueness need not rule out synergies. There can still be cooperative ventures between these self-sustaining arts groups. It is possible to create a "national local movement"—a national trend for local establishments to be formed and grow; and such a movement can promote mutual advocacy and cross-fertilization.

In 1959, a distinguished trio of theatre practitioners led by Sir Tyrone Guthrie conceived the idea to open a professional

POLITICS: ALL POLITICS IS LOCAL

theatre company outside of New York, an alternative to the monolithic Broadway stage. After evaluating offers from seven cities, they selected Minneapolis/St. Paul and in 1963 the Guthrie Theatre opened, quickly spurring a national movement toward resident professional, not-for-profit theatres scattered across the nation. (Of course, the Alley in Houston and a few other such theatres already existed.) These theatres attempted to bring to their regions a repertoire of classics, new plays, and plays with regional connections. As they grew, many of them created smaller studio stages where they could do more modern plays or those with appeal to special audiences. They developed strong bases of corporate and financial support within their communities. In some cases, they stimulated the development of smaller theatres that attracted niche audiences in their hometowns, and thus began a Diaspora of actors and other artists who now make their homes in far flung places like San Diego, Atlanta, or Seattle. The Regional Theatres today constitute a viable alternative to the New York Broadway and Off-Broadway stage. They have succeeded in creating a diverse audience for the American Theatre. Because each of them has a unique visionary as their artistic leader, and because each of them is in a different community, these adult Regional Theatres are all very different. However, as they developed, they found ways to network and support each other; and they found ways to share resources, often passing scripts, actors, directors, designers, etc. from one to another; sometimes even doing joint productions which will travel to two or more cities with essentially the same play. There now exists a thriving national circuit of regional adult theatres.

Although there has never been a New York based TYA to compare to the adult Broadway theatre, (other than touring operations that just happen to be based in New York, where there are still a large number of struggling actors available for road tours), in some ways the development of TYA companies around the nation has followed the same pattern as the regional theatres for adults. The professionalism of TYA grew rapidly in the early 1980s, with theatres springing up or switching from amateur operations in places like Minneapolis, Seattle, St. Louis, Louisville, Milwaukee, Dallas, Nashville, Phoenix, and other places. Although less endowed with resources than their adult counterparts – in large measure because of the lesser purchasing power of their primary clients—the TYA movement compensated by arousing greater passion and commitment from its new practitioners. (In subsequent essays, I will discuss many of the elements of the art form that is being shaped by these companies, and that, by the early Twenty-first Century, constitutes an important contribution to the American theatre.) Like their adult counterparts, all of these theatres developed unique personalities. Guided by the needs and traditions of their particular communities, and the distinctiveness of their respective leaders, each one developed a style, a mode of operation, and even a unique repertoire. But while the adult regional theatre movement has made it possible for playwrights and other artists to work on a circuit, moving from town to town, that phenomenon is only just beginning to be seen in the TYA circuit. One hopes it will soon increase, as the TYA duplicates other aspects of the adult theatre's growth pattern.

So far, the parochialism and uniqueness of the various TYA companies has created an interesting situation: it has become unusual to find two or more theatres willing to produce the same scripts, to share production staffs, or even marketing ideas. As a result, one finds multiple versions of the same classic tales being adapted for stages all around the country. The *Cinderella* done in Minneapolis is not the *Cinderella* done in Louisville, even though the basic underlying material is the same. There are probably a dozen adaptations of *Tom Sawyer* or *Wind in the Willows*. New plays about contemporary themes of relevance to youth are often produced only once. A playwright cannot expect to earn a significant income from having a script "catch on" on the TYA circuit, as many do in the adult theatre today. It is also not yet possible to have a career as a guest director or designer on the TYA circuit. Each theatre has its own staff or a short list of guests that it is willing to use. This makes perfect sense in terms of the local nature of each theatre's identity, but it also acts to prevent the maturation of national artists who can speak to all regions of the country—as has happened in the adult regional theatre.

I see this as the next step in the growth of the movement, and it has begun to happen in a few isolated cases. Theatres in Minneapolis, Seattle, Louisville, and Honolulu created a consortium (1989–1995) to pursue funding for new play commissions; and a few joint productions have begun to pop up, collaborations between theatres in Seattle and Arizona (2004), for example. Hopefully, this trend will grow. Regionalism and parochialism will always be there; in fact, they are a defining part of why communities support theatres. But a sharing of resources and a willingness to look at other ways of conceptualizing theatre is beginning to take place, and must grow as theatres realize the advantages of pooling resources, or nurturing artists who can develop a national presence. Loyalty to the local scene is absolutely necessary, but farsighted global sharing is also critical as the next generation is welcomed into the greater landscape of the American theatre. Like Tip O'Neill, we must retain a genuine local integrity, but learn to think and act globally.

6. AMERICAN CHILDREN'S THEATRE IN THE '80s

(The period from the mid-1960s through 1980 was one of great expansion in the arts in the U.S.A. The National Endowment for the Arts was created in 1965, and regional theatres were blossoming all across the nation, including some of today's major TYA Companies. In 1980, Ronald Reagan was elected President, and political attacks on the arts began to change the landscape. It quickly became obvious that the boundless expansion of the arts was not going to continue. In 1982, I was asked to deliver the keynote speech at a Children's Theatre Association convention at New York University, and given the charge to help reenergize our constituency for the struggles ahead. Originally delivered on August 14, 1982, the following address was subsequently printed in *Children's Theatre Review*, 1982, Volume 31, Number 4, which was published by the Children's Theatre Association of America, a division of the American Theatre Association. These associations are no longer in existence. It is reprinted here with minor editing. The risks of revealing my confident predictions for the future—as I write this note in 2005—are obvious, but I include it here as a snapshot of the status of Theatre for Young Audiences in 1982, as many of us in the field were beginning to realize that an imperative for artistic excellence was going to have to be paired with political awareness and business acumen.)

Picture, if you will, young Alice—blue dress, white pinafore––standing in the foyer of Wonderland. Perplexed. She can't go back the way she came—up the rabbit hole. Even in Wonderland you can't fall up a rabbit hole. She has to go on, through the little door. But she doesn't fit through the little door. She still carries about her the encumbrances of prosaic reality. She's too big. She has to discard a lot of "stuff" that may have served her well in Sunday school, but doesn't fit into Wonderland. She finds a potion to drink, and she drinks it. Magically, she is suddenly small enough to fit through the door and go into the beautiful garden she spies through the key hole. But then she discovers that the door is locked, and where is the key? It's up on a table she is now too small to reach.

Here we are, we children's theatre folks, who have pursued the white rabbit of Winifred Ward's dream. There was our clear vision, the vision of reaching out honestly to young people, of sharing the theatrical art, both as a process of developing the spirit of the child, and as a product to enrich the young mind and to foster a lifelong relationship between that growing mind and the changing world of art. We dedicated ourselves to that vision and we followed it into a dark and scary place, committing ourselves through a plunge into a world not totally real where none of us really get paid for what we do, and only our immediate colleagues really have much respect for our endeavors, and they're half mad. We fall for a long time convinced by Agnes Haaga's unrelenting optimism and a postwar generation of me-first children who consumed our offerings at a gratifying pace. We were on our way to Wonderland.

In the process of providing drama to a new, young, brave new world, we synthesized or invented a technique so unique we had to come up with a new name for it—so we called it Children's Drama—and the name meant fun, and a certain kind of audience, and, yes, it also meant "something less than real drama," or at least, "drama seen through special, messianic tinted glasses." But we knew that. We were willing to settle for second class status from our theatre peers and a kind of theatre that even we found vaguely sociological and educational, all because we were creating something new and we wanted to reach ALL the kids in ALL the neighborhoods, and we wanted the teachers to like us and not be threatened by our magic tricks, and we wanted to serve society, and we wanted to change the world, and these are good goals, not bad ones; and we are good people and we wanted so desperately to get into Wonderland. And the question is, did we remember to put the key in our pocket before we went crashing off to change the world, or is it still up there on some gigantic table we have forgotten how to reach? And the name of the key, of course, is artistry.

For now it is 1982. The "ME" generation has grown up and are now the young parents of what I predict will someday be called the "shortchanged" generation. The kids who flooded our theatres twenty years ago are now parents. And because they're the "me" generation, they want the best, but they want it for themselves. I'm not so sure they also want it for their kids. I suspect today's parents have a lot fewer dreams for their children than our parents did. There is serious doubt that these young kids will even grow up at all, so why spend a lot of energy on their development.

Teachers used to be highly respected and underpaid. Now they get paid, but they're down there next to used-car salesmen on the list of respected jobs. Education has become a very low priority in America and arts education is fast disappearing. Maybe it's because of the Arab oil crisis or Ronald Reagan, but the result is that the number of field trips a child gets in his or her public education has been cut to about one-third of what it used to be. Every school system from Bangor to Catalina has fewer art, music, and drama teachers than it had ten years ago.

Every level of public education is being seriously eroded up through the universities; the supposed repositories of our culture. Where do you think you can find a Ph.D. program in child drama any more in the U.S.A.? Scratch Florida State, scratch Minnesota, scratch Washington, and it is going to get worse before it gets better. The world, which for thirty years after World War II was cruising under full sail, taking us around our own globe ever faster and cheaper, and even to the moon, on live television, in prime time, is now battening down its hatches.

The storm of threatened natural resources, nuclear proliferation, energy shortages, massive public distrust, reactionary politics, and terrorism, is raging, and no one I can trust has predicted that it will end anytime soon. The fall into the foyer of Wonderland was spectacular, but the door into its richest garden is locked. And any attempt to forecast the future of children's drama in the '80s must take into account the serious winds buffeting our nation and the world.

But it is in times of distress that people turn to their inner resources for strength and for vision. I think the '80s could be a time of opportunity for those of us who serve society by strengthening its ethical values, its communication skills, its dedication, and its creative urges for a meaningful future. I predict a serious return to religion in America in the '80s, and I predict that the arts can still survive, and maybe even flourish. If children's drama can supplement its optimism and dedication with artistry and professionalism, I think it can reach a new level of acceptance and importance higher than any we have experienced until now, but it must be done in an atmosphere of reduced resources, and that means we must have quality and standards to offer, not just quantity and enthusiasm.

Already we have begun to see the influence of the economy on a revitalization of theatre for young audiences and families; and immediately we are able to see the danger of proceeding without artistry. Although it is not well-realized, our fate as children's theatre practitioners is intimately bound up with the fate of the American national theatre, which right now, consists primarily of two wings: the $30–50 a ticket Broadway experience, aimed largely at tourists and expense accounts; and the regional resident theatre companies around the nation. It seems inevitable that, as the economy gets bad, both of these wings have turned to children and family audiences to generate income. For Broadway, the economy is cyclically desperate, so it is of little surprise that it has oriented itself frequently over the years to young audiences. Think of the small percentage of Broadway shows that make money, even in good times. If you take away from that list all the fairytales and children's stories (*Peter Pan*, *The Wiz*, *Annie*, and such adult-seeming children's tales as *42nd Street* and *Guys and Dolls*) you are left with a lot of starving producers. Not only is the material of Broadway perpetually childlike, but its basic mentality seems to derive from Charlotte Chorpenning's rules for a visual, easily digestible drama.

The regional theatre of America is new enough to be going through its first real economic retrenchment, but it has found the same solution. If there is a regional theatre anywhere that hasn't done *A Christmas Carol* at least once in the last five years, it's only because its board of directors hasn't been paying attention. Most theatres have made it an annual offering, and in my home, Louisville, the local adult theatre has found *A Christmas Carol* to be so economically beneficial that it has now added *The Gift of the Magi* in its smaller space as a second regular annual offering. Ballet companies, of course, have been reducing their deficits with *The Nutcracker* for decades, and I, for one, heartily welcome the results—however mercenary the cause—if the nation's leading theatres will begin to do quality programming for young people.

But the question is: how well are they doing it? I haven't seen that many versions of *A Christmas Carol*, but based on the ones I have seen, there is a serious problem. When Ebenezer Scrooge is reduced to a vaudeville clown, cracking irrelevant jokes, and rolling his eyes, I can't help but feel that artistry has been sacrificed to exploitation. When the resources of our major theatres are finally put to the task of interpreting a great classic of literature– –and one totally suitable for young audiences—one would hope for more than camp and condescension. But, in a way, the fault is ours. Venturing into a children's theatre market for the first time, what is more natural than the adult theatres surveying the field to see what current standards and tastes are, and then striving to match them. If the models of theatre for young audiences lack artistry, and if the regional theatres are to capitalize on these audiences, it seems totally logical for them to create productions with the same lacks. The English Christmas Pantomime is an ancient theatrical style relying almost totally on "tits and ass" and eyebrows. If our resident theatres are being led in that direction because no one has shown them that seriously done artistic theatre for young audiences is a worthy and attainable goal, whose fault is that? Of course, the result is that it makes it that much harder for us. We now have the adult theatres doing camp for children, many of our own colleagues doing camp for children, the reviewers now expecting to see camp for children, and the teachers and parents– –80 percent of whom are not themselves theatregoers—unable to tell the difference between schlock and quality. Which of us are going to be able to buck that tide and insist on quality; and where in the hell are we going to find the money to pay for the difference between mediocrity and excellence?

And that of course, is a key question and it always will be. If I want to do quality work, if I want to maintain a level of artistry that meets my standards, if I want to attract serious artists to work honestly with my young audiences, if I want to commission some decent scripts, and build some magical scenery, I've got to find the money. It actually costs just as much to do good theatre for young audiences as it does to do good theatre for adults. My artists want and deserve to make a living, too. And yet, partly because of our mission, which is to include all segments of the population in the audience, and partly because of the American custom of paying reduced fares for children; the ticket prices at my theatre are one-fourth to one-third the amount that they are at the adult theatre down the road. That is an impossible situation. It is a problem that we must address and solve in the '80s. There are only three alternatives:

> Alternative 1: With current pricing and funding levels, children's theatre is perpetually condemned to a level of artistry one-fourth to one-third that of the adult theatre. We must simply accept that fact. Obviously, I am not saying that money alone guarantees artistry, but without it, the limits are quite inevitable.

> Alternative 2: We have to raise our ticket prices. Ours at Stage One have gone from 75¢ in 1977, to a high of $3.85 in 1982, although we still sell most of our tickets at group prices down as low as $2.40. That's still not enough to achieve professional salaries and production budgets. How high can we go before we begin to cut out lower-income families? Probably further than we think. The arts are not cheap to present, and we don't do ourselves or our audiences, or society, a favor by pretending that they are. Even those of us who work in amateur settings can and must teach audiences that children's theatre is theatre and it costs to go. Maybe if we become really good, and do good plays, people will want to see them enough to pay what it costs.

Alternative 3: The easiest answer to give, and the one that was probably easy to achieve until the last three years, is to raise more unearned income—more support from grants and donations. If we want high quality, and low prices, this is the only other choice we've got. But the world is quite literally against us. Two years ago the NEA abolished Theatre for Young Audiences as a category, not without some good reasons, but I must add without the slightest peep from the so-called Children's Theatre Association of America. Children's theatres now receive funding solely—at least in theory––on the basis of their quality, in direct competition with *all* theatres, which is good; but without any apparent allowance for the relative insufficiencies of their earned income potential or their lack of a body of dramatic literature with which to impress the judges, which seems a little unfair.

Now, it is a moot point, since the NEA itself is so severely under attack. All government support of the arts is going to decrease not increase, at least until after the next war revitalizes our economy. And the corporate givers are also reeling. There will be very few major grants for children's theatre in the next few years, especially since all the social services have also been dumped in the laps of these already strapped companies. If we really want to find more unearned income to support our work, we're going to have to do it the hard way—with small grants and individual donations and fundraising events. We're going to have to work at the grassroots level to sell the quality of our product, and we're probably going to still be using our educational and social relevance as selling tools. Whether we can raise enough from these sources, also increasingly overextended as tax incentives for giving are removed, and life's savings in stock portfolios reach new lows, will depend on our personal energies and salesmanship. This is not going to be the easiest alternative anymore.

Of course, even assuming we can solve our money problems, we still have some hard work ahead to find the artistry we need. But without the artistry, there isn't much reason to go after the money. Big budgets are a help, but we still need to find good actors, designers, playwrights, and we haven't done much lately to help ourselves. Last year the Charlotte Chorpenning Cup for a distinguished playwright for young audiences was awarded to nobody, since there was not a worthy recipient. This year he won again. Two years in a row with no playwright worthy of recognition—if that doesn't scare you, it should!

Last March, the Fourth Annual Showcase of Performing Arts for Young People was held in Milwaukee. In the past four years we have seen sixty-four invited companies, sixteen per year, doing a wide range of programs for young audiences—music, dance, drama, puppetry, etc. Do you know how many American scripts we have seen? I mean published plays with a beginning, middle, and end, "book" shows by American authors? Out of sixty-four, exactly two, (though we saw one of those twice, by two different companies.) That also scares me. Do we seriously believe as a professional organization that improvised revues, pleasant as they may be, are truly a substitute for the theatrical power of a well-crafted play? I begin to think we do, and that scares me most of all.

Of course, the argument is ancient and circular: you can say we will have better scripts when there are more companies willing to do them and able to do them well. It is true that there is little financial incentive to write a play if only two companies in the country do scripts. But then you can also say, we will not have any more good companies doing scripted shows until there is a body of scripts for them to do. Here's a problem I think we can solve, if we are willing, and solve in the '80s. The National Library

Association picked up children's literature by its bootstraps 30 years ago when they initiated a little financial reward for good writing for young readers. The Newbery prize is worth large sums to its winner, and the winner's publisher. Let us give a twenty thousand dollar prize annually to the best new script produced by a professional company. That's ten thousand to the playwright and ten thousand to the company. I'll bet you that in ten years we'll have the beginnings of a body of dramatic literature, and some better companies, too. Where would the money come from? The Newbery name is a household word—somewhere there's a corporation that would love to give its name to the prize. Or if that fails, raise the dues twenty dollars a year. I think a thousand members paying an extra twenty dollars could be the best thing CTAA has done in a while. Here's a project of true significance. The moral is that artistry will come when artistry is rewarded. I think it should be one of our major goals of the '80s to reward artistry.

I think, as fast as the world is changing, the field is changing, too. If you go to the Annual Showcase you'll learn a lot more about what's going on in theatre for young audiences today than you will by sitting here listening to me. I think some things are happening, and I think you'll see them if you go. I think in the '80s you are still going to be able to tell that our roots are oriented to the PROCESS of drama. There will still be improvised shows, there will still be street theatre; there will still be audience participation. But I am hoping that there is also going to be a new legitimacy of PRODUCT. I think in the '80s, it's going to become respectable to be a professional artist who works for young audiences. I think it is going to become respectable to do an expensive beautiful production with real scenery and stagehands and $15 ticket prices. It's going to be respectable to hire the best New York actors to come to your city and play the roles in this play, and turn on your audiences; and that means it is going to be less respectable to hire twenty-two year-olds to play all the fathers and mothers, and I guess that will mean that they will have to wait a little longer and develop some more artistry before they're good enough to play for young people, and so be it.

Interestingly enough, I think there is also going to be a new legitimacy given to the creative visions of young people. I think it is going to become perfectly respectable for young people to be playwrights, designers, and even actors if they are disciplined enough to have that artistry. I think that Meridee Stein's and Nancy Niles Sexton's work with young actors is totally legitimate, and I think the Young Playwright's Festival—where the works of teenage and younger writers are being given serious attention – is going to change the way some of us think about children as artists and as audience. I think Steven Spielberg has done more than any man lately to give legitimacy to the visions of children, and I hereby nominate him for the Monte Meacham Award. There is no better antidote to Ronald Reagan's neanderthal view of the world than to see the world through the eyes of a child, and Spielberg's child characters see the world, both sacred and profane, that is our best hope for the '80s, and maybe our only hope to survive into the '90s.

I think we have had it pretty easy up until now. What is easier than following the rainbow, than falling down the rabbit hole? I think now it's going to get tough. I think, in fact, that we are going to be fighting for our lives. I think the economy is against us; I think our reputation for mediocrity is against us; and I think our own subliminal and subconscious fear that maybe we really are second class is also against us. I don't think it's true. I think insecurity is always going to be with us, but that's not necessarily bad, because after all, "Security is mortals' chiefest enemy," and

I would rather go down – if go down we must – like Brutus for love, than like Macbeth for doubt.

So let's commit to being a little insecure. Let's commit to standing up like professionals to be counted, even if it costs a little something to stick our necks out. Let's commit to keeping our vision—long our sole support—our vision through the keyhole and into Wonderland. But let's also commit to a new thrust toward standards, towards excellence. As Sara Spencer would have said, "Let's stop leaning on our shovels." To use the metaphor of the moment, let's scramble up the sides of the table and grab firmly the key marked artistry, and find the money, and develop the talent, and open the door, and go on into the garden.

THE ART OF THEATRE FOR YOUNG AUDIENCES

THE ART OF THEATRE FOR YOUNG AUDIENCES

7. ON EPHEMERA

The experience of attending a live theatre performance is so different from almost anything else in a child's life, that it is amazing to see how quickly he or she understands it. With the possible exception of attendance at parts of a church or synagogue service—with which it has more than a trivial common ancestry—-there is nothing in a child's life that prepares him for the theatre, and yet the theatre grants instant access.

There are certainly similarities with other activities, the cinema, television, or a sporting event; but none of these are quite the same. The cinema and television are not live. If one were to watch the same film or TV program a dozen times—and children do love to repeat experiences, wearing out a favorite DVD or book with daily repetition—each time it is exactly the same. (That is, no doubt, one reason why children love to repeat, they gain the power to predict the outcome, which is rare in their young experience.) In the media experience, one is very cognizant that the event is not live. It is on a tape or disc or book. You can hold it in your hand, insert it into a machine, or carry it to your grandma and ask her to read it to you. You have control of it. You have less control at a cinema, but you are still aware that it is not alive. You can come back tomorrow and watch it again, with no variations. And, most importantly, the actors are not really there. They made the film many months ago. The performances are finished, complete, perfected, canned.

A sporting event is happening in real time, and the outcome is not completely predictable. The athletes are performing now, as we watch, and the event's conclusion depends on their present actions. But a sports event is a game, and not a story. There are frequent interruptions while a coach gives instructions or replaces players. And there is a basic similarity to all of the games, a defined set of rules, a limit to the game's length, set by actual elapsed time, or some other format such as number of innings played. In a sporting event, the same rules generally apply at the beginning, throughout the middle portion, and the end of the game. And there are usually two or more competitors with a very specific goal where one, and only one, of them ends up as the winner. There may be a sense of drama, in that suspense and excitement are generated, but there is no sense of story. Watching sports can be exciting, but it is not the same as watching theatre.

Children coming to the theatre for the first time are often confused. They will say things like, "When is the movie going to start?" They do not know about the conventions of the stage, such as house lights going down, or curtains going up. They have never seen anything to compare with theatrical lighting effects. And they certainly have no experience of an actor playing a role and addressing them directly. And yet, they invariably go along with the events as they unfold. They seem to have an innate understanding of how to watch a play. If the play is produced in such a way to engage a beginner's skills at watching, they will absorb it all. In the next essays, I will discuss ways to match theatrical presentations to the child's level of aesthetic development. But first, let us think about the very nature of the theatre, or other performing arts. It may be useful to define some general concepts; to agree on what constitutes a theatre experience; on what makes it nearly unique.

Theatre is ephemeral. It is happening now, in real time, and we cannot rewind it, freeze the frame, or slow it down. We can watch the same play again, but it will not be exactly the same; and I have noted many times that those children who watch a play two or more times can instantly identify detailed differences between the performances. It is often their first question after the performance: "Why did you change that?" Having grown used to the predictability of a recorded performance, they are quite interested in the concept of a mutable one.

Theatre is also happening *here*, in the presence of the spectators. Not only can we see and hear the actors, but they can see and hear us! You can't do that at the cinema! We even have the power to affect the performance. If we laugh loudly, the actors will pause in their speaking until they think we will be able to hear the next line. If we cheer for the arrival of the hero, we can sense that he is encouraged by our approval. If we hiss at the villain, he may even glare at us. If we lose interest in the performance, that will also affect the actors and they may become louder, or even angry. But if we do become involved in the story and perceive the characters as real human beings, and care about what happens to them, there will be an energy transfer between us and the artists, and the entire experience will become additionally charged with emotion and empathy.

Moreover, the art experience is basically a perceptual experience. When we respond to a piece of flat canvas covered with pigment, as if we saw an ocean storm, and become emotionally involved in the fate of the tiny ship blown about by the waves, that is an art experience. There is no ocean, no ship. The artist has arranged stimuli on the canvas to give us the *perception* of a storm. When we respond to a theatre performance *as if* we were seeing characters and not actors, *as if* the story was taking place in front of us for the very first time, and the outcome was unknown until the denouement, we are having an art experience. The characters are fictional; they never existed. The lines are memorized and rehearsed. The denouement is well-staged and controlled. The ushers know exactly when to open the doors at the end of the play. *Art is when we respond to something that is not there as if it were, all the while knowing that, in reality, it is not there.* We call this "the willing suspension of disbelief." We agree to follow our perceptions instead of reality. We allow imagination and emotion to guide our behavior instead of observation or detachment. (This principle applies also to the recorded variant of theatre, to television dramas or films.) Of course, there is some small reservoir of truth in our consciousness as we watch. Even as we believe it is real, we simultaneously know that it is not. Later, we may be able to analyze our own responses, having divided ourselves into two creatures—one believing, and one aware that we are pretending to believe (or suspending non-belief.) The "suspension of disbelief" can also be stopped by many things: a fire in the theatre, a sudden opening of a door letting in daylight, or, sadly, a weak performance that fails to inspire believability. But, primarily, we agree to follow our perceptual journey through the play.

Therefore, the play takes place in the mind of the observer. The actors can perform the carefully rehearsed sequence of actions, with appropriate attention to subtext. They can even believe in the emotional truth of what they are saying and doing. But the play is not what happens on the stage, it is what happens in the audience's minds. The perceptions are the art work. The performance is, for the most part, a carefully orchestrated set of stimuli, just as the distribution of oil pigment on a flat canvas is the set of stimuli provided by the painter, but the aesthetic event takes place inside the audience. Moreover, it is likely that, since everyone brings their own history and associations to the event, every individual in the audience experiences a slightly different play. We may even assume a situation where different people in the audience identify with different characters. I might think of myself as the hero's sidekick, while you are empathizing with the hero himself. A parent and a child, sitting together, might have vastly different experiences of the play, especially if the play's theme involves an intergenerational conflict.

Because the play takes place inside the mind of the audience member, one can never say that a response is "wrong." We artists can do everything within our power to make sure the stimuli presented—the visual production, the behavioral nuances of the actors, the studied delivery of the text – are all exactly as we intended them to be; but it is up to the spectator to complete the message, based on his or her own perceptions, prejudices, and attitudes. (Later, in the essay on acting for children, I will remind you of this point. An eighth grade boy who responds to a strong display of emotion by laughing is not "wrong;" he is applying his normal defense mechanisms to an important, unresolved, emotional need of his own.) Audience members, in each individual's own way, are experiencing exactly the right play, based on the stimuli provided, for them.

There is also an important communal response to the play. I respond to my perceptions, with my associations and identifications, and you, sitting in the next seat, respond to yours, and *we are aware of each other's responses*. I find a line of text funny and the child next to me does not, but we are sharing the moment, so she learns something about me and I learn something about her. She breaks into belly laughter at a bit of slapstick business, while I only smile reluctantly at it. We do not stop our journey with the characters to learn about each other, it just happens in the background. As a result, we feel as if we have shared something special, something that happened here and now, but also that gave us each a glimpse into each other's history and personality. The same kind of bonding can also happen at a sports event, although there it tends to reinforce a similarity between us. In the theatre it can do that, too; but it can also reinforce a "different-ness" between us. With some small part of their awareness, audience members learn how other audience members respond differently to the same stimuli, and how, at other times, they respond similarly. These feelings multiply and make us feel like a part of a group, yet with certain unique qualities that make us special. In the case of a school-time performance with teacher follow-up, or a family performance where the parents initiate a non-threatening discussion, we also get to analyze those feelings, and mature a bit in our self-awareness. But self-awareness isn't necessary for this process to take place. As in all other areas of life, children absorb knowledge, community standards, ethical understanding, and human experience just by living. Exposing them to the right experiences is how we raise our children; talking about it afterwards might add insight, but the learning goes on anyway.

As artists, we try to control the stimuli we are presenting to the audience. To the extent that our resources and talent permit, we carefully choose scenic elements and costume colors. We cast just the right actor, and develop the relationship between characters through movement and textual interpretation. We try to make the story clear, and the protagonist someone about whom we care. But since the individuals in the audience are responding to their own perceptions of the event, and since the reactions of their neighbors becomes part of the pattern of stimuli to which each of those individuals is responding, it is evident that the experience will vary widely from day to day. Because the audience is different, the reactions are different, and therefore a subtly different event takes place. Of course, these audience variations also affect the actors through the energy exchange that always takes place. This communal response varies from performance to performance, and even when the actors are studiously recreating exactly the same performance, the differences in the audiences will, by itself, ensure that no two performances are alike. In the TYA these differences can be remarkable—public audiences and school audiences are poles apart; fourth graders and sixth graders can enjoy the same play in totally different ways; there is even a difference in sophistication and socialization between a first grade audience in the fall and the same audience in the spring after several additional months of schooling.

The artists stimulate, but cannot control the audience's mental processes. We may like to assume that everyone processes information—including the stimuli provided by theatrical artists—in much the same way. But that is simply not completely true. Past experiences also affect how each individual responds to the play's stimuli. If a particular color reminds a certain child of an unpleasant experience, even subliminally, that child may not respond to the character wearing that color in the way we might predict. If a child has experienced a traumatic event, perhaps a fire in their home, that child is liable to become agitated over a fire simulated on the stage, and that agitation might have nothing to do with the play's story. Moreover, if the person in the row behind us is distracted, or needs to talk out loud about a moment in the play, those stimuli also become a part of the play experience for us, and affect our perceptions, and our mental processing of the play.

A child's way of processing information from the production is also affected by mental processes, or habits of processing information, that may occur away from the theatre experience. If one watches a lot of television, for example, one develops the expectation for stories to be acted out in seven-minute segments, to allow for commercials. There is possibly also a limit to a person's attention span, although I find that attention increases rapidly as interest or danger mounts. (See also Chapter 18.) Still, the "commercial break" phenomenon is one to which we may become accustomed by exposure to a certain technology. Other types of technology also affect mental processes, as we begin to develop expectations for controlling our media experiences. For example, with some technologies one can stop the action of a story, rewind it, and watch it again and again. One can fast forward or skip actions. One can zoom in or out to change one's perspective view of a scene. One can click and drag a bit of data, or send and receive instant messages, perhaps commenting on what is going on in class, or what one thinks about while watching a film. All of these manipulations of the process of telling a story act to change it from an ephemeral event to one that can be controlled, paused, and repeated. In effect, one has the ability to dictate the timing of a story. But in the theatre, one cannot stop time. The ephemeral nature of our art form may challenge the expectations of a technologically sophisticated audience, and that might frustrate them. Or it might be a welcome return to a more natural state of experience—bound up inescapably in time as it passes (just like our own lives)—and that may, in fact, be a part of the continuing attraction of the live theatrical event.

Since each audience member has a different set of experiences, and a different set of associations to bring to the encounter with the play, we cannot completely predict how any individual will respond to our performance. All we can do is try to understand how a child's mind might work under most normal situations. The more we know about the stages of development in normal children, the more we understand how aesthetic development takes place, the better we can be at predicting a general pattern of responses to our work. Then we can refine our understanding by carefully watching audiences as they do respond.

8. THE CHILD AUDIENCE: TOWARD A THEORY OF AESTHETIC DEVELOPMENT

(Originally printed in the *Children's Literature Association Quarterly:* Fall 1984. Permission obtained for reprinting, with minor editing.)

During the past twenty years, I have observed around a million children attending theatrical presentations of one sort or another, from child performers attempting to impress their peers and parents in barely audible school assembly programs, to the world class artists of the famous Theatre for Young Spectators in Leningrad [now St. Petersburg], the visually stunning confections of the Minneapolis Children's Theatre Company, and the heartrending emotional truth of smaller professional companies from Czechoslovakia to Seattle. I have seen the old favorite titles––the Cinderella's and the Alice's—in dozens of interpretations, with budgets from zero to hundreds of thousands of dollars. I have seen children who saved their allowances to buy tickets, and those who were dragged off by parents or teachers, sometimes not even knowing where they were going or why. I have seen tears of laughter, and heard gasps of real pain. I have seen enough to convince me that there is something going on in that often darkened space when the performers repeat their lines and the audience tries to believe them.

The paragraphs which follow are not based on research, but on observation and intuition. My object is to form an understanding of a phenomenon I call "aesthetic development." By "development," I mean those changes in the individual organism which bring it from one level of ability to another, presumably higher, level. While "aesthetics" is much harder to define, I use the term to mean the ability of the human mind to respond to stimuli that aren't there as if they were. When we see a canvas depicting the full power of an ocean storm, we make a response that is cognitive: we recognize the scene; and emotional:

we feel the power. Yet there is no ocean before us, it is merely pigment arranged carefully on a flat canvas. Somehow we have supplied enough information from our memory or imagination to complete the process begun by the person who arranged the pigments, the artist. This active mental process by the viewer is the aesthetic process. It can immediately be seen to be a process, like most mental processes, which allows for a range of individual differences, and which is subject to development.

Artists arrange stimuli; audiences perceive stimuli. The aesthetic process mediates these perceptions; the audience experiences something that was perhaps intended by the artist. But in the theatre, the stimuli are provided by whole teams of artists, and are of a complexity that approximates a real-life situation. We get human behavior, language, locale, music, costume, symbolic use of properties, and other kinds of content. We get them all simultaneously; and we get them in real time, with no chance to go back and review. We are generally attending to one set of stimuli at a time, and we do so knowing that we are thereby missing other stimuli. If we watch a speaker to see how her behavior corresponds with her language, we cannot usually also watch a listener to evaluate his reaction to the words. (It is one of the stage director's main functions to ensure that the attention of the audience is directed to the onstage event of greatest import.) Because of this complexity, the advantage of developing aesthetic processing skills to a theatre audience member is significant; but the same complexity makes it hard to study this development. Only recently has a reliable instrument been created for categorizing the responses of children to theatre. While this instrument, as described by Patricia D. Goldberg ["Development of a Category System for the Analysis of the Response of the Young Theatre Audience", *Children's Theatre Review*, 32, Spring 1983], should make it much easier to identify steps in the developmental process, we must rely on observation to try to understand how the child develops these processes.

If there is some truth to the notion that ontogeny recapitulates phylogeny, it should be useful to review some key stages in the development of the Western theatre from primitive cultures to today. Theatre seems to have grown out of the same basic human need as religion, and theatre and religion together took shape in primitive society as magical ritual. By acting out the capture of the buffalo, the primitive hunter increased his chances of actually catching one the next day. Let us call this first phase "Acting Out." We mimic events and behaviors to influence them. Later, we mimic them to remember or celebrate. Still later, we may develop a kind of shorthand, such as the Catholic mass, which remains a symbolic reenactment of specific events that took place two thousand years ago. The creation of this *symbolic* re-enactment to replace a detailed imitation of life leads directly to the next phase, the Classical period of theatrical art.

The Classical style was also heavily religious in its origins, and evolved as a means of worshipping a particular Greek god, Dionysus. The god was worshiped by enacting philosophical debates illustrating the choices which the worship of this particular god demanded. To enliven the discussions, the two points of view were put into the mouths of two different characters. Thus was created the first "scene." The creation of a third speaking character introduced the possibility of three sides to a discussion. One side was "right," the other was "wrong." What could the third side be? It was at this point that religion and the art of theatre diverged.

Since the enactments of the Classical style were symbolic instead of mimetic, it was necessary to develop a language of symbols, so the audience could understand what was going on. This language we now call "theatrical conventions." The Greeks developed elaborate rules to determine what could and could not happen onstage, what kinds of events could be symbolized as opposed to other sorts which could only be reported.

In the middle ages, theatre tended to remain conventional and stereotyped; but in the Renaissance, many individual artists determined not to be bound by conventions. Of course, by defying rules, they only created newer, more flexible rules. Marlowe, Johnson, and Shakespeare led the way in England; others in Western culture— especially the Spanish writers—were equally creative in evolving a freewheeling style that could encompass years and continents in the passage of an instant. If an actor remarked on the circling seagulls, the audience was transported to the coast. If he carried onstage a torch, it became night. No longer content with the Classical "unities" of time, place, and action, the Renaissance theatre constantly challenged the audience to keep up with a world of "as ifs" that were fixed only by the language of the play.

Although I have called it Renaissance, this period of development really didn't end until the 1880s; and one of its most important statements came near the end of that time, the sub-phase called Romanticism. This period saw the introduction of fanciful scenery, which made it possible for playwrights to change the rules by having someone pull on a set of hempen ropes. But the main reason I group Romanticism with the Renaissance phase is that its statements glorify the freedom of choice and the worth of the individual. Shakespeare wanted the writer to be free to create his own rules; Hugo wanted the characters in his plays to be similarly free. From 1550 to 1880, then, the dominant theatrical development was an expansion of, and a challenge to, the rules—

in spite of an occasional reversal, like Neoclassicism.

The next phase, Realism (and its extreme form, Naturalism) may seem to be a step backwards from the free expression of the third phase. Audiences go to the theatre and expect to see real furniture in a real living room, with real characters drinking and smoking and talking of real, even mundane, things. Of course, even reality is a convention in the theatre. The water may run in the kitchen sink, but it runs into a plastic tub under the sink—the pipes are only real when they can be seen. Nevertheless, there seems to be less unstructured freedom in this period, and that in fact is its contribution. The theatre of this phase substitutes our own lives for the symbolic lives of kings and queens, or abstractions of good and evil. This theatre is about us. Beginning in the 1880's with the works of Ibsen and Chekhov, and justifying the creation of a whole new theatrical sub-field, the cinema, the theatre has become a tangible means of examining our daily lives. From being a magical way to manipulate the outside world to obey our commands, the theatre now became a way for the outside world to manipulate our expectations. To the extent that we define our goals and aspirations by what happens to our favorite character in a situation comedy, our lives are influenced by our theatrical surroundings.

There is a fifth phase in the development of the theatre, but we are barely into it, so it is difficult to describe accurately. Nevertheless, its shape grows clearer every year. This post-realism has no official name as yet, but I tend to think of it as Eclecticism. In every previous age of theatrical history, when plays were done from prior periods—and that occurred only rarely—they were changed into a format acceptable to the contemporary society. Shakespeare rewrote the Romans, the Victorians rewrote Shakespeare, and Hollywood has rewritten the Victorians. But in the last thirty years, a theatrical phase has begun which permits works of every age to be done in a way that at least attempts to be historically accurate. We now find plays of Sophocles, Shakespeare, and Shaw performed simultaneously. The National Theatre of Great Britain might be performing all three in the same building on the same night. One result of this Eclecticism is that choice has returned to the theatre. We may select an experience for ourselves that is appropriate to our state of mind of the evening. Another result is that we can see and study the whole range of theatrical development without leaving our hometown. Individual expression for the theatre artist is a benefit, too. A playwright like Arthur Miller can use realistic and expressionistic conventions in the same play; primitive ritual reenactment can occur along side romanticism or absurdism. Perhaps this freedom of choice and this blending of past experiences represent the highest stage, or perhaps a sixth, unimagined, lies ahead; but these first five stages, admittedly an oversimplification of theatrical history, do prove very useful in examining the development of theatrical aesthetic process in the individual child.

"Acting out" corresponds to the child's first dramatic inclination. Children learn much of their social behavior by practicing it, first in the crib, then in their own homes, and eventually, in the schoolyard. Until language skills are well-developed, it may be their best way to learn. The desire to play out moments, behaviors, conflicts, dialogue, etc., is innate, and all humans play. Whether children do so to magically influence the world around them, to learn its ways, or to savor new discoveries, I cannot tell, but I expect it is for all three reasons, and others besides. Children at this age really do not have much aesthetic sense. In order to have an arts experience, they have to recognize the difference between life and not-life. By definition, there can be no aesthetic awareness until the thing is perceived as not really there. Toward the end of this phase, at around age three or four, when children are substituting other means of learning for mimicry, they can begin to delegate the responsibility for playing out the events to an actor/priest/medicine man. At this point they are ready for their first theatrical experiences. (Any age references are intended to be comparative only; children vary in aesthetic precociousness as much as in athletic ability or intelligence.)

The second phase of aesthetic development involves learning rules, learning that they are rules, learning that they are rules because the artists made them up and might want to change them someday, and most important, learning that we control the aesthetic event by choosing to believe or not to believe in the rules. (Or better perhaps, as Coleridge says, to "suspend our disbelief.") The child from four up to seven or eight is certainly learning social rules. It seems in keeping with Piagetian notions of overall development that this would be the period when the absorption of aesthetic rules also takes place. Among those rules which the child needs to learn, some stand out as basic:

- The difference between the "stage" and the "non-stage," i.e., the actor pretends to be a Witch while he is in this certain physical space, when he leaves that space he is quite able to return to his own identity.
- The temporary nature of character, i.e., when the actor stops pretending to be the Witch, the Witch is *gone!* (Later, of course, we learn that the Witch existed only in our own aesthetic process, and was never really there.)
- The use of costume to indicate a role.

There are many such conventions to be learned. One trend in theatre for young audiences involves presenting this age group with so-called "participation plays," which involve them at certain moments in the play in vocal or physical actions necessary to the completion of the play. This forms a nice bridge between the child's "acting out" stage and the "learning the rules" stage. Children participate at moments in the play so that they will learn that there are other moments when they are not supposed to participate. At the same time, they are usually witnesses to all the actors' preparations, and see them make certain adjustments in location, vocal quality, costume, physical stance, and so on.

The third phase of theatrical development also corresponds to a stage in the child's aesthetic growth. This is the expansive Renaissance stage of challenging the rules and overthrowing the boundaries. The child aged eight through twelve is the one who falls out of trees trying to fly, and explores new frontiers in his or her own backyard. This child understands the existence of the rules, but wants to try out different rules. There should be more than one way to do things, and in the theatre, there is. For this age group, the eclectic potential of today's theatre is also most appropriate. By experiencing a Balinese dance/drama today, and a *commedia dell'arte* comedy tomorrow, children quickly learn that there can be more than one set of rules. This fulfills their notions of what ought to be, so they begin to expect each play to set its own conventions. This is the ultimate meaning of the concept of style, and mastery of this concept culminates this phase of aesthetic development. The lack of such mastery is one of the major obstacles to the development of a strong national theatre in this country. Too many adult theatregoers have never received the exposure required to teach them to process varying conventions.

If the third stage of development has been neglected by theatres serving adult populations, the fourth stage—reality—has been ignored by too many of those that serve young audiences. Young audience members must learn that the theatre can influence their life. A play can be about a thirteen-year-old afraid of not growing up, or about a youngster who can't fit into his or her peer group, or about one with a physical or emotional handicap, or about one with parents that reject him or her.

These things matter, to a greater or lesser degree, to all children between eleven and fifteen. Never again will an audience in the theatre be as homogeneous in regard to what is bothering them as they are during these ages. The theatre must present them with an opportunity to learn a new kind of aesthetic process, applying vicarious experiences to their own immediate situation. This phase personalizes the art form. Up to now, the theatre has dealt more or less with forms of expression, now it becomes relevant to their lives. Nothing could be more damaging to the developing aesthetic sense than to continue to present eclectic conventions with little relevance. These will drive the children from the theatre. Many theatres that serve youngsters stop at age twelve; some youngsters eventually find their way back as adults and complete their development, some never do. As with literature, it isn't enough to create child readers and hope they will become adult readers. Somehow we have to make the child readers into teen readers; and thence into adult readers. But if the theatre can provide these experiences, young audience members will absorb them and continue their development into the final stage.

As there is something we call physical maturity, and it represents the culmination of physical development, surely there must be something called aesthetic maturity, the culmination of aesthetic development. Maturity represents a reaching of potentials, an arriving at a level which, for our genetic structure, is as high as we can go. I assume that the goal of all education is to help all individuals to reach their personal maturity in all areas of development, including aesthetic development. It is for this reason that I place so much stress on school systems providing arts experiences corresponding to the theoretical scheme I am describing (or some verifiable alternative). If our society is not evil or bankrupt, it seems to me that its first obligation must be to provide a system that enables individuals to reach their fullest potential. There can be no higher goal. But how then can we define aesthetic maturity? How will we know when the average child reaches it, and what are the ranges that less gifted and more gifted individuals should reach? These parameters are defined for physical growth. Are they for aesthetic growth?

The significant factor in the fifth stage of theatrical development is choice. Today's Eclecticism provides it. Maturity as a theatregoer means choosing freely from the available range of experiences. There is theatre for escape, theatre for political consideration, theatre for intellectual challenge, and theatre for recreation. All are valid; none is an inferior form to the aesthetically mature.

For youngsters fourteen and older, assuming they have followed the development scheme up to this point, it really isn't necessary to do special kinds of plays. It might be good to introduce plays from the adult repertoire that are of particular relevance to youth— *Romeo and Juliet* would mean more to them than *King Lear*, perhaps. There is also a body of great plays that deal with major ethical issues that society has faced at one time or another, and these plays—important to all members of a society—might well be introduced at this time, if a theatre for young audiences wanted to perform that additional service. But no special theatres should be necessary for this age group. There is a reason for one to exist, of course, if the sequence has not been completed, and the youngsters have not had a chance to learn about the variety of conventions or the relevance of theatrical works to their own lives.

The principal implication of my argument that aesthetic development generally repeats the pattern of the development of theatre art is for theatres for young audiences. Those of us concerned with the development of this process in young people are required to make choices about the kinds of plays we present, and most critically, for which age group we present them. To produce realism for children with limited aesthetic awareness is to repeat the mistake of television and the cinema, and force growing children into the belief that only one set of conventions exist. On the other hand, to neglect realism, or at least realistic problems, in plays for the teenage audience, is to force upon them the notion that theatre is irrelevant to serious people. Yet plays are selected with much less rationale today by many theatres; my theorizing does provide some basis for an approach to play selection.

But it would be a horrible mistake to assume that all one had to do to develop aesthetic processes in individuals was to expose them to plays in the order recommended. The most basic, first concern is that the plays be *good*. Aesthetic learning takes place indirectly. No actor comes to the forestage and says to the audience, "Now, notice that when I pretend to die in this scene, it is only the character that is dead." The child learns this convention very quickly, assuming he or she has reached the phase of development when he or she is ready to learn it; but he or she learns by getting involved in the emotional truth of the moment, not by being lectured to. Yasha Frank, an instrumental shaper of the Federal Theatre Project back in the 1930's said, "Children love to learn, but they hate to be taught." If the play is well done, the acting honest, the dialogue convincing, the costumes well-executed and appropriate to the character, and all of the other components of the play harmonious and skillfully made, then children will become absorbed in the world of the play, empathize with the characters and their problems, and learn. If the play fails in one or more of these facets, children will quickly become aware that they are being "taught." There is no greater enemy to learning.

Like the child reader, the child audience represents a potential, not only as new human beings on the developmental trail, but as future citizens/consumers/leaders of society. If we believe that literature and theatre art can be valuable additions to our lives, necessary components if we are to reach our fullest potential, we have the obligation to foster the development of the right processes in new generations.

9. THE STAGE, BY STAGES

The previous essay was written over twenty years ago and intended for a readership of librarians and others interested primarily in children's literature. It provides, perhaps, an intellectual foundation for describing how a process of aesthetic development might occur, paralleling the evolution of theatrical forms. It does little, however, to illustrate how these concepts might be applied, or what actually seems to occur in a young audience of various ages as they watch a play.

Childhood is not a monolithic event, and children change rapidly as they pass through it. Each person has a unique journey to make through the years of childhood, and—like snowflakes—no two journeys are exactly the same. But stages of that journey are often similar for individuals of the same age. Those of us who attempt to provide meaningful experiences for these travelers must always be prepared to focus on the individual child, and listen to his or her particular questions, and answer them specifically and appropriately. But there are common issues and shared experiences as these individuals pass along their journey. We can serve many of these common needs by addressing theatrical experiences to specific age groups. Nearly all children will pass through key landmarks on their journeys, and many of them will do so at approximately the same age, plus or minus a month or a year or two.

Each play is also a unique event. It has a story to tell, and it tells it in a special way. Themes support the storytelling, and a theatrical style illuminates the way of telling it. But plays also cluster into types and genres. Certain themes repeat, with variations, and certain styles are favored by some artists.

The suggestion, then, is that it might be possible to produce a certain type of play for a certain age group, and have it resonate in an effective way with a critical mass of the individuals in the audience. Moreover, it might be possible to structure a sequence of theatrical experiences, so that the productions aimed at one age group tend to prepare them for the productions aimed at the next highest age group, and so on, until the audience arrives, both chronologically and aesthetically, at maturity.

I like to describe the stages of aesthetic development as if they were discrete, specific events geared for specific ages with specific goals. But theatre experiences almost always bridge over more than one stage, containing elements that are more youthful, as well as some that are more mature. And most of the children in the audience will be ahead on some aspects of development, and behind on others. Nevertheless, it is useful to consider several distinct phases in the audience's development, as if they represented general tendencies. In any given population of children, a large number of individuals will cluster around similar developmental stages at about the same chronological age.

The pre-theatre child creates his or her own plays. Most of them seem to be imitations of things around them. They imitate the speech sounds of their parents, and that's one way they learn to talk. As they get older, they try out more and more complex behaviors, once again tending to imitate the models around them. If the family has a pet, they will act out the dog or cat as readily as their parents or siblings. The element that defines their play as a pre-theatre experience is role playing. If they make speech sounds because the mother makes speech sounds and they are trying to become the mother, then, at some level, they are role playing. If they move as the dog moves because they are pretending to be the dog, that is dramatic play. At a later stage, they will manipulate objects, assigning roles to them. By three years of age, they are creating puppet plays using their dolls, or stuffed animals. These plays may not have a plot, they may not have conflicts or resolutions, but they play out behavioral sequences, and practice relationships and other behaviors. It is an easy transition for these children to see other people manipulating puppets, perhaps in more complex behaviors, although plot is still not a necessary element for this age group. This age group is also starting to watch television, hopefully experiencing positive learning models through a program like *Sesame Street*, once again in short vignettes. Ideally, they have been introduced to the book format at a very early age. Parents or other adults have been reading to them, and they learn to interpret the pictures they see in the books, and how to appreciate a story for the first time—a plot that has a beginning, a middle, and an end or resolution. At about age four, they are ready to put these pieces together—role playing; objects acting out roles, (i.e., *others* as role players); pictures that tell stories; and plots with a climax and a conclusion. They are ready for the theatre.

As a transition into the live theatre, I recommend the Participation Play. (Since this is one area in which I have considerable experience, I will devote the next essay to discussing, in more detail, where the Participation Plays came from, and how they work.) This is a chance for the audience to move from a younger stage, where the children are (themselves) doing the role-playing, manipulating the characters, and/or making up the action sequence in imitation of the models around them, to a stage of delegating the role-playing to others—to the actors. All good theatre is participatory; the audience should always be empathizing actively with one or more character. They should always experience tension in their bodies at moments of crisis. They should experience joy at a comedy's successful resolution and pity at a tragic hero's fall. The energy of their participation should be palpable to the actors on the stage. But the adult audience should not feel like they are controlling the action themselves. In fact, nothing makes a mature audience uncomfortable about a performance as much as a feeling that the actors are not in charge. For the young child, acting it out themselves is the normal pattern. They now must learn to surrender control of the story to others. By giving them a chance to participate at key points, and then not participate at other key points, they begin to see the difference, and begin to learn how to participate aesthetically, instead of actively.

There are many other learning opportunities in a Participation Play, and this will be the subject of the next chapter. But, hopefully, by the end of their exposure to this format (perhaps at age seven; although it could be sooner if they get to see plays more often than the annual field trip that the typical school provides,) they are skilled at delegating the role-playing to the "experts," they expect to sit back and enjoy the play as vicarious observers, as aesthetic participants, but not as active participants.

The second phase of theatre for young audiences (TYA) can, in some ways, be the richest and most accessible. For the child from approximately eight to approximately eleven, I recommend an exposure to a great variety of theatrical styles, and a great many of the traditional tales of childhood, both in traditional stagings, and in those that challenge expectations. In many ways, these are the core years of childhood. The young person has enough language, motor, and social skills to participate in life. They can read some, hold a discussion at a certain level, and perform complex tasks such as playing a sport or baking a cake. And yet there are few pressures on them. Their bodies grow gradually, with none of the hormonal gyrations that will affect them after age eleven. American society places few onerous expectations on this age group, other than that they get along with their peers and continue to learn at a moderate pace in the school setting. There are also many joyous opportunities. Many wonderful books, films, television programs, and other activities such as theme parks and summer camps seem to be geared especially to this age group. This can also be a time when they enjoy a rich variety of experiences in the TYA.

It is important to take advantage of the fact that this age group still has no strong expectations about the theatrical event. They are willing to accept any set of conventions that the theatre artists can provide, as long as there are enough clues for the audience to decode the rules of this particular production. Any production concept can work, if it is revealed in a clear way. People can play animals in a variety of ways, for example. They can try to realistically walk on four legs, and speak only in animal noises, or they can be entirely human with clothes that suggest animal coloration, and perhaps a trace of an accent in their speech that suggests the animal's vocalizations. They can paint animal markings on their faces, or wear wimples with ears. Children will accept any of these variations, as long as the production is consistent. If the "animals" don't speak, the play may be entirely narrative. In other styles the characters may sing and dance—itself a very conventionalized approach to plot development; the audience will go along with whatever the choices are. They are still of an age that has faith that what they are being shown is right, so they accept it, learn it, and enjoy it. Adults, and children as young as eleven may challenge this license, saying, "That isn't the way it is supposed to be done," but most children eight through eleven are happy to take whatever artistic journey we can bring them on. This is, therefore, an opportunity to let them see the full range of theatrical styles and genres. I would program fantasy, adventure, magic, realism, tales from many cultures and continents, serious and comic styles, musicals and straight plays, and of course plays drawn from all the many books that this age group is reading. For the artists, this is an exciting age for which to perform because it is a chance for them to test their own creative ranges. Literally nothing within the comprehension of the audience is out of bounds, at least not for artistic reasons. If I can imagine a way to tell a story theatrically, and be clear and consistent in introducing it on the stage, this audience will accept it eagerly.

By experiencing all these various genres and styles, the audience is also broadening its knowledge of the theatre. They are getting to see stories from many cultures brought to life in the theatre. They are noticing that there are many ways to tell a story in the theatre. They are appreciating that the artists they love to watch have an enormous range of expressive styles in the theatre. This exposure helps to create a lifelong awareness of theatrical possibility. These audiences are less likely to turn into adult theatregoers who are puzzled by experimentation or unique creativity. By stretching our own wings as artists communicating to young audiences, we help to ensure that we will be able to experiment and grow as artists later on when we work for these same individuals as grown up audiences. Plus, we are having an enormous amount of fun by reliving this golden period of childhood when anything is possible, and belief is still alive and strong.

As the child enters the next period, things start to change, both internally and externally. Typically, ages eleven through fourteen are accompanied by shifts in self-awareness, and the beginnings of shifts in power between the child and the adults in authority. These changes are often accompanied by mood swings, self-doubts, blind adherence to peer pressures, and/or wild pushes for independence. This age will start to reject the theatre if the theatre remains fixated in earlier modes. Animal tales lose their appeal to a child coping with self-esteem issues. More than anything, this young person is trying to escape the label of "child." He or she is trying to find out who they are, and how they fit into their group of peers. Although they may swing back and forth between needing a parental guide and wanting to succeed without one, they do not want to be thought of as "children", or do anything that children do. In 1978, when I became the Producing Director of the Louisville Children's Theatre, one of the first things we did was change the name of the theatre. We wanted to play for young people in this age group, so we took the word "Children" out of our name and became "Stage One". (The field as a whole made a similar decision shortly afterwards, adopting the term "Theatre for Young Audiences," and dropping "Children's Theatre" as our designation.)

For this age group, I recommend programming that deals with young people experiencing the very same psychological and social issues that the audience members are experiencing. The plays may be historical—such as *The Diary of Anne Frank* or *Huck Finn*; or they may be contemporary – such as Cherie Bennett's *John Lennon and Me*. They do not have to be strictly realistic in style, but they must treat the problems of the protagonist in a recognizable and realistic way. The characters may even be stylized or exaggerated, as long as the issues are bona fide issues of adolescence. The goal is for the child in the audience to accept the fact that this play is about "me or somebody I know." The contemporary pre-teen or teenager does not literally expect to be a Holocaust victim, or help a runaway slave escape, or contract a potentially fatal disease, which describes the situations in the three plays mentioned above; but, in all three plays, the teens act like we would act if we were in those situations. This creates a believable relationship, and there are immediate applications. While none of us are Anne or Huck or Star, we might have experienced arbitrary constraints, or unfair discrimination, or a close contact with illness. These plays do relate to our lives, and we accept that these characters *could* be us, if we were in those situations.

A wonderful assortment of books for this age group exists. Many talented authors have created believable teens or pre-teens with emotional problems to solve, with important questions of identity, with issues of peer pressure, or self-image and self-esteem. At Stage One, we made a concerted effort to identify some of these books and have them adapted for the stage. Working with novels by Avi, Madeleine L'Engle, Katherine Paterson, and others has opened up a treasure of potentially exciting dramatic literature, and many other theatres in the field have also been tapping into these sources of good material for this age group. There is also a genre built around heroic fantasy that appeals equally to this age, such as the Harry Potter books or Spider-Man—but note how much of those stories are concerned with exploring the self-doubts and peer pressures on their protagonists. Masquerading as fantasies, those tales are emotionally valid explorations of adolescent angst that are easily accepted by readers and theatregoers as appropriate for ages eleven and up.

Theatres that do not wish to do these kinds of plays should not try to program for children above age eleven. It may be possible to convince middle school students that they will enjoy plays about witches or talking animals, and, indeed, there are some few teens that still do retain a childish delight in these elements; but my belief is that these kinds of experiences actually alienate most teens from the theatre, convincing them that "theatre is only for children."

If a young spectator has had high quality exposure to the previous three stages of well-focused plays—Participation Plays from ages four through seven; a rich variety of conventions and genres from ages eight through eleven; and plays that make a transition to "theatre about me" from ages eleven through fourteen—then by age fourteen he or she is ready for most adult theatre. There are, however, still some wonderful experiences that such a spectator can have in a specialist TYA, if it does an occasional play from the adult repertoire that deals specifically with issues relating to youth. *Great Expectations* or *Romeo and Juliet*, for example, are classics that can be enjoyed by adult audiences everywhere, but they have special resonance for high school students and—as long as there is no stigma of attending a "children's" event attached—can be meaningfully presented as a fourth phase of evolving an adult theatre audience by a TYA company. Another important reason for doing so involves the artistic growth of the artists attached to such a company. The opportunity to tackle this challenging material offers enrichment and opportunities to stretch which help to retain and develop long-time company members. In addition to all of the satisfaction that we might take from presenting wonderful plays for young people, it is also good to occasionally prove ourselves as equal to the task of producing adult material, especially if it also stretches the audience.

I believe that there is one additional phase of theatre that can be legitimately presented by the TYA, and that is the so-called "Family Theatre," or a single theatrical presentation that attempts to present something for all ages. These plays exist, although they are much rarer than many might think. One often encounters plays that are marketed as suitable "for all ages." Often they appeal to adults because the adults are enjoying observing the responses of the children next to them. This kind of multi-age appeal should really be present in all of the plays done, at all of the phases discussed above. Children are almost invariably brought to the theatre by a teacher, parent or other caring adult. Of course, that adult wants the children they have brought along to enjoy the experience, and of course, there is a very real, vicarious pleasure to be found when, in fact, the child does enjoy it. But there is also the possibility that a play may have enough levels of meaning and expression that different age groups in the audience can take away different emotional and intellectual messages, can actually experience the theatre on totally different levels, but simultaneously. Sometimes this can happen because of a play's interpretation. The staging or physical action may be enough to enthrall a young child of four, while the text carries a mature meaning for the adult. A lively production of *A Midsummer Night's Dream* might very well enrapture all ages from four to ninety-four. At other times, it may be that the story is both allegorical and immediate, so that young people can respond to it as a simple tale, but adults can perceive it as an allegory. *The Wind in the Willows* has both animals acting out on a physical level, and important moral questions about managing change in our lives. These kinds of plays also provide artists with great opportunities to enrich their own creativity, and so should be included in a theatre's repertory when possible.

Over the past decades, as I have been trying to implement

this approach to TYA—to explore a "developmental theatre"—I have had a chance to observe thousands of audiences as they respond to productions. There is no such thing as 100% predictability, I am still surprised occasionally by the responses of an audience, especially a volatile school group. But there are many elements which are predictable. Almost always, an audience of predominantly five-year-olds will take great delight in the moment when the villain realizes he has been defeated, more so even than the moment of his defeat. Nine-year-olds, on the other hand, can predict the defeat of evil, and will find great enjoyment in each step of the struggle as the climactic scene unfolds; for them it is worth prolonging the moment with suspense, as they can anticipate much better than their younger counterparts. For a thirteen-year-old, I might choose not to show the actual defeat of the villain onstage, but rather to imply that it will happen, or even to make it ambiguous. This age group finds satisfaction in working out the clues, on deciding how it will end on their own. In a similar way, one can often predict how the audience will react to a bit of slapstick, or a strong expression of friendship, or a verbal joke. The more one understands the stages of a child's development, the more one can provide suitable stimuli, moments that reach out to that level of aesthetic understanding. But there is no certainty in audiences, and I continue to learn by observing them as they respond to the performances.

Obviously, experiences outside of the theatre influence the way individuals and groups respond to the theatre experience. Childhood is also evolving. Things that were common to five-year-olds, now seem to target four-year-olds better, and leave five year olds feeling somewhat bored. Adolescence seems to arrive earlier and earlier, and the concept of a "tween" age group with special needs and interests has arisen in the last ten or fifteen years. Frequent exposure to theatre can also accelerate aesthetic

ART: PARTICIPATION THEATRE

development. Six-year-olds who have seen more than three or four Participation Plays may be ready to move on to plays where they do not have to join in the action physically. As a nation, we have seen changes in the rate of development in many other areas. Children are more socially mature at age ten in the twenty- first century than they were in the mid-twentieth; they may also be larger and stronger than their parents were at any certain age. Exposure to high quality arts experiences may be helping them to mature earlier in aesthetic awareness.

10. PARTICIPATION THEATRE

My concept of Participation Theatre is still evolving. That tells me that there is no one perfect way to do it. Older variants seemed effective, and the newer experiments also seem to work. Other writers and directors have come up with totally different approaches, and many of those succeed, as well. The descriptions that follow, therefore, are only one possible starting place. The goal is to produce a theatrical experience for very young children—four through seven-years-old, perhaps—that starts out by capitalizing on their natural instincts for playing along, teaches them at certain times during the show how to delegate the playing to the actors, and also introduces them to certain critical conventions of the living theatre.

My first exposure to this format was through the published plays of Brian Way, the British playwright, who was actively producing Participation Plays for young audiences in central London, and also, with Margaret Faulkes, training teachers in the use of drama in the classroom. All of Mr. Way's productions were performed in the round, with the audience seated on the floor surrounding the action. Audiences were strictly limited in numbers, so that the actors could effectively communicate with each individual in attendance. His work was unique at the time, and several of his plays had made it into print, and across the Atlantic. I directed his play, *Mirror Man*, at Southwest Texas State University in 1966, and showcased the production at a Southwestern Theatre Conference, where it drew great interest. Subsequently, I attended a summer workshop taught by Mr. Way in London and came back to this country with many ideas on the strengths of his approach, and also some ideas of my own on ways to refine it.

Mr. Way was using this format for all ages up through eleven, or even older, but in my observations the older children seemed to be somewhat patronizing of the actors. While the younger children were participating with full commitment, the older ones seemed to my American eyes to be slipping into very polite British reserve. I sensed that they wanted to not participate, but felt like they had to go along with the rules of the game. However, there was definitely something appealing about the methodology. My conclusion was that direct audience participation could best be used in a transitional phase as a means of separating the functions of player and audience; and so best suited for the child just learning about the aesthetics of theatre.

Early in my exploration, I sensed that many threads of theatrical history were bound up in this distinctive format. It contained echoes of the earliest primitive ritual reenactments, when tribes gathered around a group of performers who danced and acted out the hunting of the antelope in order to magically influence the success of the next day's hunt. One can imagine that all of those present were stepping to the rhythms of the dance, but also acknowledging the superior skills of the shaman/dancer, on whose prowess their very survival depended. The spectators were simultaneously a group of eager participants, and an audience of worshipful believers. Centuries later, Brian Way was capitalizing on the modern audience's continuing passion for the storyteller. By bringing them into the enactment, he was making them an active part of the ritual.

Many of the tales that seem appropriate for Participation Play treatment are archetypal explorations of human relationships. This subject will be explored further in the next essay, but it seemed to me even in my earliest experimentation with the format, that we should capitalize on the universality of these themes. There is nothing trivial about the stories we are telling. They are about big subjects, like parents and children, finding the self, or falling in love. The themes suggested parallels to the early Greek plays, when human passions became personified as gods and goddesses. For example, the Witch is an important expression of human greed and power, and she is also a psychologically relevant personification of one aspect of the Mother. I sensed the importance of keeping these plays honest, of telling them as allegories of human passions and relationships. Whether scripted in advance by a playwright, or developed creatively in rehearsals by a company—and I have done it both ways—the connections to archetypal forces should never be ignored.

I also saw a connection between this format and the *commedia dell'arte*, in the days when strolling players improvised in the town square, and the townspeople stood around their raised platform with a rowdy appreciation of the skills of the artists. Here was an immediate theatrical form, seemingly created on the spot, and yet embodying stock characters and set speeches when they could be used effectively. I was persuaded that one could use a similar style to show the young audience how plays were done; that we could actually recreate the experience of a troupe of players arriving, setting up a stage space, putting on their costumes and characters, and acting out a story in a way both familiar and new.

Another tie, especially in the visual production, was to the Asian theatre; for example, the use of a branch to represent a tree, or a flag to represent an army, or an "invisible" *koken*, dressed all in black, to move the scenery or hand a prop to the actors. The young audiences I wanted to reach were quite comfortable imagining their environment during their own expressive play. Here was the theatrical equivalent. Why depend on elaborate scenery and props, when the audience was eager to accept the premise that a cube could be a throne in one scene, and then magically transformed into a tower? The child's imagination could be one of our tools in creating this type of theatre. As the style developed, I was gratified to see the children's drawings, done after their theatre experience. We had used a cube and a small door of bars to indicate a jail cell—they drew a complete cell; we had used a single branch to represent a forest—they drew dense clusters of trees. Their visual 'memory' supplied all of the details, as I had hoped. Older children and adults may need to be shown the pictures, but this age group seems used to providing them from internal imaginative sources. At that point, the only scenery we were using consisted of a wooden prop trunk, usually set in one corner of the stage area, and two or three cubes, built so that they could nest inside one another. With the addition of a few props, the cubes became all the locales the story required. The audience invariably understood, and supplied the pictorial background from their own imaginations.

In the beginning, I focused on familiar stories. I wanted to introduce—to teach—the elements of live theatre, and to guide the young audience to a new kind of aesthetic participation, a substitute for their natural creative and/or imitative play. If the plot was already known to them, I thought it would highlight the *new* aspects of the experience. More recently, I have tried the format with lesser known or original stories, and it can certainly work with that subject matter, but as I was also learning how to use a new set of conventions, it helped me to deal with familiar plots and characters.

I also theorized that, following the *commedia* model, it would be possible to present many different stories with the same set of actors. I believed that a small number of lines of roles could tell many, many stories. From the first experiments, they became almost a "universal cast." There were two juveniles, male and female. They could play all of the young characters, who were almost always the protagonist—Hansel and Gretel; Jack and the Giant's slave; Aladdin and the Princess, etc. There were two more mature character actors, also male and female. They played all of the parental roles, plus the kings and queens, the genies and the fairy godmothers. The fifth actor was assigned all of the villains – the ogre, the witch, and the giant. While all of the casting was critical, this actor had to have the right blend of threat and non-threat. He had to convince us that evil was a force to deal with, but not be so scary that the young audience turned away from the play. It was usually possible to create a villain that one could also laugh at, but the laughter must never negate the danger, or the hero's accomplishments would become trivialized. The final member of my early troupe was the mime. Drawn from the Asian *koken*, this character played the role of the *theatre* itself. Anything that we didn't have with the first five actors, the mime would have to supply. She could change the set, she could hand props to the other actors as needed—always invisible to the other characters who seemed to receive the prop out of thin air; and she could act out all the other utility roles in mime—the herald, the dragon, the spinning wheel, etc. With these six actors, we could tell almost any story. Later, primarily in order to save two salaries, I reduced it to as few as four. A good many of the tales didn't really need both parental figures, one was usually enough. And we also found ways to do without the mime, although some sense of theatrical magic went away with that omission. Seeing the actors move their own set about, or find a prop in a box or trunk was practical, but I missed the mystery of the silent character. Moreover, the mime was almost always the audience's favorite. After the show, she was the one that most of the kids wanted to meet. They wondered if she could really speak. ("She never does.") They identified with her apparent vulnerability, yet she possessed great power as the one who gave out the implements that enabled the other actors to tell the story. Although the four and five actor scripts have proved highly successful, I still believe that six is a better size for a "universal" company. The extra actors also helped in the creation of the play's music.

A key component of these plays was always the music. From the first rehearsal, it became the actors' problem to figure out how to bring the play to life, including the music. In the *commedia* troupes of old, the actors did everything themselves without stagehands or technicians. Almost all of the Participation Plays have songs in them, as another facet of the theatre for the audiences to learn about, but also as a way to bring variety and change into the storytelling, and to allow the characters to expand on their relationships, dreams, worries, etc. We almost always included a brief overture to introduce the music, and to introduce the very concept of an overture. In the case of the overture, all of the actors played some instrument; otherwise the actors who happened to be offstage during a song were responsible for accompanying the singers. Ideally, there would always be at least one actor with musical skills in the company. They could play a keyboard, or some other melodic instrument. In the worst case, when none of the actors were talented in that way, we used kazoos and a simple xylophone as accompaniment. I have also resorted to having the music director lay down a track on a synthesizer, and then one of the actors could pretend to be playing the instrument while the prerecorded music accompanied the song, but that seemed a bit like cheating. This style of theatre needs versatile actors. They should be able to sing and dance and play an instrument and juggle and play a wide range of roles. They also have to improvise well in a pressure situation, as we will see later in the discussion of the audience participation moments. The rewards to the actors are also great. They get to use all of their skills, and they get to play every performance for a most appreciative, most demonstrative, and most engaged audience that is sitting literally inches from the action.

The physical venue for the Participation Plays has also been carefully thought out. The best space is simply a large square room, at least 40-feet by 40-feet, although larger is better, and with a floor comfortable enough to sit on. Ideally, the acting area is in the center of the room. I like to use a 16-foot square, which can simply be marked out with ribbons or strips of wood, or it could be a slightly raised (two to four-inches) platform. In the four corners of the acting square are aisles marked on the floor, about three-feet wide, and leading back about eight-feet towards the corners of the room. One of the four aisles—the one designated as the actors' staging area or orchestra pit for the accompaniment —is a bit wider, perhaps. The children will sit on the floor facing the stage area. I recommend limiting the audience to *no more than 250 children*—the maximum number that will fit into about five or six rows on the floor. That is also the largest group that the actors can reasonably expect to communicate with effectively, and it keeps each child within arm's reach from either the front or back of the seating area. Behind the audience on the floor is an unmarked passageway, so that the actors can move freely behind the children. Behind that passageway, on all four sides, perhaps up against the wall of the room, are chairs for teachers who do not choose to sit on the floor, parents, or older children who may have come along with their siblings.

   Seating the children as they arrive could be done by the actors themselves, or by friendly ushers. The goal should be to make some kind of eye contact with each audience member. All children in the right age group—typically four through seven – are urged to sit on the floor. Adults who want to share directly in their experience should also be encouraged to do so. Children younger than four who want to sit on the floor may be permitted, if they are with an older sibling or parent. Children older than seven, especially if they have experienced this style of theatre several times, will frequently not want to sit there. They should be treated like the adults, and offered seating on the chairs. The play begins with a prologue, discussed below, concluded by an overture, and then the main story. An observer with a view of the entire space will probably witness a most interesting phenomenon. There will really be two separate events going on in the room simultaneously. The central area consisting of the stage and the children on the floor becomes the acting space for the Participation Play. In effect, since they are active participants at certain points in the story, the floor seating space becomes a part of the stage at times. The floor audience should be totally absorbed in telling the story, and actively involved. The second event impacts only the chair audience. They are seeing a cooperative and seemingly improvised play, performed by the actors and the floor audience together. Although the chair audience should also be engaged, they are more removed from the story telling. Their experience is more nearly one of observing the skill of the actors and the involvement of the child participants. They should feel like they have been let in on the inner secrets of the process. They have the power to appreciate the way the story is told, and the way the children become involved from a more detached position. Since they should already have made the transition from active participation to aesthetic participation, the performers are not asking them to regress and help tell the story, but rather they become collaborators with the producers—enjoying the way the children are involved and sharing in their delight from a distance.

After the audience is seated, the actors, if they have not been doing the actual seating, come out to meet the audience. I call this activity the "pre-prologue," and it is totally improvised by each individual actor, working with a section of the audience. In the *commedia* concept, each actor has created a persona as an actor, as a member of the acting troupe. At this point, he or she may not seem to know what today's play is going to be, or what role they will take. All they know is that they, and their fellow company members, who may have complicated relationships among themselves—as acting companies often do—are here to do a play, and this is today's audience that must assist them. The play's written Prologue may give clues to these relationships, and often those relationships foreshadow the interactions between the characters in the story that will be told, but the actors are still free to elaborate and explain to the audience just who they are, and who these other folks are that will soon be doing the play. There are three goals in the pre-prologue: to establish rapport with the audience, to introduce at least one of the actors in a more intimate way to each part of the audience, and to establish any safety rules that may be necessary. The actor must try to make eye contact with each child in his section of the audience. He may ask questions of the audience about their trip to the theatre, or their past experiences. He may tell them something about himself, or show them a warm-up exercise he likes to do in preparation for acting. Regarding safety, he may warn them about keeping fingers off of the stage and feet out of the aisles, since the actors will be stepping close to the edge of the acting square, and running in and out through the aisles. Since the audience is divided into four sections, at least one actor should take one whole side of the floor group. After a couple of minutes, the signal is given to move into the scripted prologue. If the theatre is using stage lighting, perhaps the signal is simply the house lights going out, but lighting is certainly not required in this format, and I have often produced it in the middle of a gymnasium, or even outside. In that case, the signal might have to come from a waving stage manager, or just from one of the actors loudly calling an end to the chat with the audience.

Now begins the scripted prologue, which I have almost always used in Participation Plays. Considering that these plays often last an hour or less, I think it is important to devote ten minutes or so to the activity of preparing to do the play. This is where the audience learns about the live theatre, how it differs from television or film, how actors use intention and emotion to reveal characters, how the scenery and props will be handled, how imagination may be used to create a locale, what the use of costumes signifies, etc. Ten minutes may not allow for every aspect of preparation to be shown with every play, but those elements most important to this particular story can be covered. Following a format similar to the one used by *Sesame Street* on television, I have always created a series of short scenes, always involving some conflict, which makes the scenes dramatic in some way, and often also exploring the relationships between the members of the acting company. (These traveling actors—the troupe—are, of course, being played by human beings. That is a level below the "play within a play," and may not be instantly perceived by the youngest members of the audience. But the chair audience knows, and it adds to the strata that make up their theatrical experience, as opposed to that of the floor audience.) If one of the actors is doubling, i.e., playing two or more characters during the story, this is a good time to have him deal with how he will distinguish the two—perhaps by a costume change, or a different physicality. Two elements I have *always* included in the prologue: an introduction to the villain of the piece, and an introduction to the actual active participation of the audience members. In order that the youngest children not become too frightened when the witch or ogre appears during the story, the prologue gives us a chance to watch the actor putting on the role. The moment may involve choosing a scary mask and letting the audience help in making the choice, or it may involve one member of the troupe helping another to practice a scary walk or an evil sounding voice. The audience clearly gets to recognize that this is an actor playing a role. Hopefully, this allows them to have an aesthetic experience of the villain during the story. He becomes an essential, and even frightening part of the tale, but he is a part of the tale, and not, therefore, a threat to us in the real world. Audiences also need to practice once themselves for their later role as helpers. In this same vignette, or in a different one, it must be established that at certain moments the actors may need help. A pattern is established for how this help will be solicited, and the audience should make a verbal commitment to helping later on if needed. The prologue ends, ideally, with the announcement of "The Overture," and after it is played, the story starts.

Although we have gone to great pains to teach the audience that these are actors playing roles, once the story starts, theatrical skill and seamless performances should follow. The company must sell themselves as now being the characters, for only when the plight of the characters is believable to the audience can good theatre take place. Hansel and Gretel must truly be hungry; Jack must truly have faith in the Bean Seller. And even if the villain seems comical at times, he must represent a believable threat. The characters reveal their dreams and fears through action, or sing about their feelings. They engage each other honestly, and they listen carefully to each other's problems. Whether the story is enacted from a published script or a company-developed improvisational scheme, it must seem to be happening now for the very first time, and it must ring of verisimilitude. For many in the audience, this will be their very first experience of live theatre. The stakes are too high to allow "camp" or insincere acting to infect their young appreciation of this powerful art form. And when, during the enactment of the story, their help is needed to move forward, the need should be real. The protagonist must be in a situation where, without a genuine commitment from the audience, he or she must fail.

Good audience participation sequences include several characteristics. Of course, there must be a genuine dramatic purpose to the participation. It has to *move the story forward*, either by revealing something important about one of the characters—usually the protagonist; or it has to solve a problem that the protagonist, or his helper, is experiencing. Moreover, it should *allow for a creative solution*. The audience can easily be manipulated into responding to a direct question, such as, "Which way did he go?" But the goal of participation should be to draw the individual audience member into the play by allowing them to become, for the moment, actors. The task of the moment should be something that can be done in a unique way by each child. "Use your whole body to become different kinds of pastries," or "Think of an ending to the poem. Think of all different kinds of endings." Later, we will find a way to recognize at least a few of the most original or creative responses. Finally, the participation task must be something *that can be done safely from their places in the audience*. The audience can become seeds and grow into beanstalks, or they can tie their ropes to their neighbor's ropes, or respond vocally with a possible rhyme to complete a poem, but they should never be encouraged to move from their places. That would create a dangerous situation for both the audience and the actors.

Each planned audience participation falls into five distinct components:

First, the characters must establish a real need. Hansel and Gretel have to fill up their basket with berries, or they can't go home. And there are no berry bushes anywhere. When Beauty's father locks her up so he can go and kill the Beast, she doesn't know how to get out. The Beast will die if she cannot get out and save him. The audience must believe that the protagonist has a serious problem that cannot be solved without outside help.

Second, there must be a clear understanding of what the audience might do to help. The idea can come from the actors or from the audience. Gretel might say, "Can you all use your whole bodies to become berry bushes?" Or they might ask the audience for suggestions and then pick one, repeating it clearly so everyone understands the same concept. Beauty can ask the audience, "How can I get out?" The first clear idea she hears becomes the concept. It might be, "Break the window," or, "Make a key." She restates it clearly, perhaps even elaborating on it, "We all have to make keys. One of them is bound to fit."

The third component is the signal to begin. "When I count to three, everybody make a different key. One, Two, Three!" This ensures that everyone will begin to perform at the same time. It prevents the shy kids from hanging back, and it also keeps the dominant kids from showing everybody else how they are supposed to do it, because the goal is always to have every child "do it" his or her own way. Later in the play, if the audience has participated several times, they may not need this signal; they all may start playing as soon as the task is clear. In this case the actor should cut the signal lines. The last thing you want to do is get behind the audience. If they are ready to go on, they should.

Fourth, the actors should reward creativity and originality. A few of the best participants should be pointed out and praised. "There is a really interesting berry bush!" "Oh, I can tell the berries on that bush are really heavy." This doesn't need to take too long, but perhaps one child from each of the four sides can be recognized in some way. In certain participations, it may even be good to ask them what they are doing. In my adaptation of *Rumpelstiltskin*, the Baker and his daughter need the audience to become all different kinds of pastries in order to impress the Queen. They might divide the audience in half and each ask the most interesting shapes what kind of pastry they are, and then comment on how wonderful, or delicious they look.

Fifth and finally, the need has to be resolved. "Oh, we have plenty of berries now!" "The key worked! I'm out!" Almost invariably, when the actors announce that the need has been met satisfactorily, the audience will stop playing and return to their position as spectators. If they are so wound up in the playing that they don't hear the line releasing them, simple hand gestures, or a repeated, "Thank you, we have all we need," will get them back into audience mode.

Because the convention has been established that the audience can help the actors, it sometimes happens that they want to help at unplanned moments in the script. They may sense a need that the characters have, and they may decide, on their own, to offer assistance. Since one developmental goal of these plays is to have the children not participate sometimes, but let the actors handle it, unplanned participations should never be encouraged. But they will happen sometimes. This can be one of the trickiest challenges in doing Participation Plays, and it is one reason why one should always use the strongest actors possible. I have always believed that, if a *significant portion* of the audience wants to participate, keeping faith with our own conventions requires that we accept their offer. A single child, however, should never be accepted as a significant portion of the audience. There will be many individuals who will shout out a suggestion or a solution to a problem. The actors should ignore those and move on briskly. But if other audience members pick up one of those solutions and begin to insist on it, or if, spontaneously, a surge toward participation begins in several parts of the audience, then it must be incorporated. This requires that the actors improvise the moment. Sometimes the suggestion merely accelerates the action in the script. In these cases, it may be possible simply to cut some dialogue, and get to the exact moment that the audience is calling for. At other times, it may be necessary actually to try out their suggestion, and have it fail. It may be necessary to have an offstage actor enter, to move the plot forward. The play *Rumpelstiltskin* is particularly challenging, because the final third of the story depends on the Princess not knowing the little man's name (she desperately needs his name to save her baby) and the *audience already knows the name*. If they care at all about the Princess, they will almost always tell her at some point. In fact, in my script of this tale, I describe seven points in the play when they might tell, and provide possible revisions in the text that can be rehearsed in advance. Most of the alterations involve the return to the stage of Rumpelstiltskin, who then informs her that she also has to guess his *last* name. For other unplanned participations, remember the sequence of five components. They have already found a need or they would not be proposing to help. Clarify the task, give a signal to start, reward the best efforts, and then resolve the need. If it is critical to the play that their suggestions *not* work, and the need is not satisfied, the entire company must be prepared to make instant cuts in the script to get to the moment in the play when that particular need *will be* addressed. The audience can become quite insistent if they think the characters are still in trouble.

There is, fortunately, one trick that will quiet down an audience for a few seconds so the actors can regain control and move to the next critical point of the play. Any new physical action will require them to pay attention until they have absorbed it. It should be something unrelated to anything that has gone on before. For example, a pesky mosquito could invade the set. Or an actor can enter and try to do something physically demanding. The audience will get quiet for a few seconds, and then the company must jump to an important action, or the resolution of the need that the audience is clamoring about. This new attentiveness will only last a few seconds; it should not be wasted on getting in a clever joke or a bit of exposition. The actors really need to have a grasp of the plot structure, and know where to go next to insure the audience rejoins them. Many of these plays have been company-developed, so the actors already know how they are structured, and what the next critical "beat" has to be. But even a fully scripted play should have some improvisation in it, if only the parts that involve the audience—who, after all, has not been at any of the rehearsals.

When the last needs of the protagonists have been met, the play should end. This age group intuitively knows that the drama is over when the conflict is resolved. Since there was a prologue to introduce the idea of "putting on a play," there should be an epilogue that tells us we have finished the play, and now we have returned to being actors. This may be simply taking off the costume pieces that were added to create the characters in the

ART: STORIES AND STORYTELLERS

first place. Or it may be a simple poem to thank the audience, and suggest that they applaud if they liked it. For many of these children, it is their first exposure to live theatre. At least once someone should teach them how to recognize the efforts of the actors.

Participation Theatre is a self-limiting phenomenon. It attempts to teach young children the fundamentals of live theatre, and help them to separate live theatre from recorded media. It also should allow them to distinguish between moments in the play when their active help was needed, and other moments when the characters' needs were met without their help. After a few exposures, they are ready for a more traditional type of theatrical experience; one that continues their theatre education by exposing them to a wide range of styles and genres. But the seeds of lifelong theatre appreciation may be planted here. It is a form that challenges actors to their fullest concentration and honesty. But it delivers immediate rewards for the acting company and the potential for a life of arts enjoyment to the audience.

11. STORIES AND STORYTELLERS

At the center of the village is a small park, with a clearing and some stools and benches. There sits the village storyteller. Around him the villagers gather often, and he tells them stories with animation and expression. The stories are entertaining, of course. There is humor and suspense. When he starts to speak, all of the villagers who can possibly get there are sure to be listening attentively, for this is one of the few respites from the constant need to search for food and shelter. For an hour, they can lose themselves in a vicarious adventure, in an escape into another world. But this storytelling is also a serious business. There are characters worthy of emulation, and others that frighten, or

111

make the listeners laugh. And underlying it all there is a tradition that defines the village. Some of the stories are cautionary tales—they show the consequences of improper actions. Others are chronologies of great ancestors, or inspirational role models. Perhaps some tell of the nature of the gods, and others of the foibles of foolish creatures. Taken all together, the stories form a cultural heritage. As a body, they represent cultural literacy. The way people act in these stories teaches the village how to behave.

To be a village storyteller conveys a certain privilege, but also a certain responsibility. Assuming that the elders of the village see a value in a culturally literate society—one that knows and follows the accepted moral code of behavior—they will nurture the storyteller, and provide him with a comfortable chair, and food from the harvest. The storyteller, for his part, has an obligation to help build a contributing society, by carefully presenting for his listeners the appropriate role models. But when danger threatens, and especially when changes in behavior may be necessary in order to ensure that the village will survive and adapt, then the storyteller may be placed in opposition to the very leaders that have protected him. He may, indeed, be the one most able to show new paths to the community, to help them evolve in new directions by expanding on the repertory of stories that he tells.

In the modern world, the same functions may fall to the theatre for young audience (TYA). We may be required to build cultural literacy; to produce the plays that reinforce traditional values and give a context for our current society. Or we may need to envision the future needs of an ever-changing world, and give our audiences the role models that will empower change, and new ways of behaving. I believe it is also possible for us to achieve a blended function, where we can tell the old tales, and preserve the old cultural values, but simultaneously tell them in such a way as to allow for an evolution of behaviors into a newer pattern. How can this be? Can a story be both traditional and forward thinking? Perhaps it can, because human passions and needs have not changed, but the way we go about to pursue our needs has. Elemental emotions are a constant, but society's behavioral customs evolve. From a playwright's point of view, the characters in many good plays have elements of the archetypal in them, but the particulars of their situation are what make them believable as characters.

The collection of folk and fairytales that make up a significant portion of the dramatic literature for young children (under seven or eight,) seem to come primarily from oral tradition. They have been literally preserved by village storytellers, and retold countless times. But each time they were told, I imagine that the storyteller made subtle variations that pointed up morals for his particular time and place. Doubtless, he chose which story to tell, and which conflict to explore based on specific needs of his immediate audience. And that is what we do today when we adapt and readapt traditional tales into theatrical scripts. We try to make them relevant. This is more or less what Shakespeare did when he took familiar tales from Holinshed or the *Decameron* and made them relevant to Elizabethan society. And it helps explain why so many adaptations of the same familiar tale are done by TYA Companies today. Each artistic director or playwright sees a different value in the tale, or a different need in the community they serve, and so they seek to bring out that message as the play is shaped.

Theatre also has the power to mean more than one thing at a time, because human behavior can be ambiguous. In real life, it often happens that we are not certain what our parent, or significant other, or a complete stranger meant by "that remark."

The behavior of others is frequently confusing, and sometimes we debate a person's intent for a very long time without reaching a definitive conclusion. An action in a play can be similarly debated. What exactly is Hamlet trying to accomplish by pretending to be mad? Thousands of actors have interpreted his actions in thousands of ways. In fact, it is almost a truism in the theatre that the better a play is, the more it yields to various interpretations. Perhaps one of our goals in the TYA should be to present young audiences with behaviors that are not always clear, but that require some analysis to understand, or, in fact, that admit of more than one interpretation.

One of the inspirations in my own work on fairytales has been *The Uses of Enchantment*, by Bruno Bettelheim (New York: Vintage Books, 1989). Bettleheim writes from a psychoanalytic viewpoint about the importance of allowing children to make their own interpretations of fairytales. He almost questions the value of staging them as plays, because he thinks that the choices made in staging will remove the child's opportunity to infuse the tales with his or her own need for meaning at that time in their lives. As an example, I think he might hold that because a very specific actor is cast as the Stepmother, it diminishes opportunities for a child to imagine a different physical type as that character in his or her own inner struggle. Bettleheim's position seems to be that the stories must be told, not read, and ideally by a parent or significant adult, for the child to get their full value. In this way the child can take from the tale those elements for which he or she is most ready. The fact that a parent is telling the tale also conveys permission for the child to use the tale in analyzing relevant psychosocial problems. The critical processing of the tale is done inside the child's mind, which is just where the processing of the performing arts takes place. I like to think that Bettleheim would be more accepting of theatrical treatments of these tales if he understood just how playwrights and directors are able to present human behaviors with their ambiguities preserved. If he could have experienced a well-written, well-acted dramatization, I think he might acknowledge that there was still much left to the audience's interpretation. I do not know what his exposure to the theatre was, but many of his assertions about inner processing seem to me to be directly applicable to the young audience at a good production. In fact, early in his book, Bettleheim gives a set of goals for the fairytale that could easily become a creed for the TYA practitioner:

> For a story truly to hold the child's attention, it must entertain him and arouse his curiosity. But to enrich his life, it must stimulate his imagination; help him to develop his intellect and to clarify his emotions; be attuned to his anxieties and aspirations; give full recognition to his difficulties, while at the same time suggesting solutions to the problems which perturb him. In short, it must at one and the same time relate to all aspects of his personality—and this without ever belittling but, on the contrary, giving full credence to the seriousness of the child's predicaments, while simultaneously promoting confidence in himself and in his future.

An important element in Bettleheim's endorsement of fairytales, especially for younger children, is their universal optimism. Every tale, and every drama, requires a meaningful conflict. Cinderella is treated badly, and suffers unjustly. But she wins in the end. You may interpret Cinderella as a virtuous young girl who befriends mice and wins simply because she is good; or you may interpret Cinderella as a young girl who internalizes her abuse and, like the classic battered child, believes somehow that she deserves to be punished; and only wins at the end because she is made to realize that it is not her fault, and that she is worthy of love and happiness. In either case, the key point is that she does win. The story teaches the child that even the most downtrodden victim may overcome evil and live "happily ever after." Playwrights who choose to adapt this classic tale have a full range of options available to them. They can choose a theatrical style, they can choose a level of psychosocial realism, they can add in elements of magical assistance, or internal struggles to find self-worth. It is still Cinderella. It can still show human behavior as complex and hard to pin down exactly. It can show possible conflicting reasons for actions, or play them as elemental forces with little explanation. It is still Cinderella. There are still opportunities for audience members to confront their own internal fears and project their own needs. Complexity and ambiguity allow for individuals to interpret the dramatic event. But it is still Cinderella, and it has a happy ending, at least for the worthy characters.

A principal function of childhood, according to Bettleheim, and others, is the constant search for meaning. Children want to learn the way their society works, and how to behave in it. They want to learn how to conform, and sometimes they need to learn how and when to rebel. Theatre can be an important place for them to learn these things, just as the clearing where the storyteller told his tales was important for our ancestors. And the old tales—constantly reinvented—can be one source of material for these lessons. But there are also new tales that can be told in the theatre, both tales adapted from new sources, such as novels, films, television programs, even video games; or tales that are created specifically for the theatre.

The best new tales also allow the audience to interpret for themselves what they might mean. They might include a fundamental optimism, although as the children in the audience get older, universal optimism loses some of its believability. A realistic conclusion might show hopefulness, but not necessarily an easy win for the protagonists. As the adolescent continues in the search for meaning, an understanding of compromise comes into play, and "happy endings" can seem forced and unacceptable, knowing the way things usually turn out. But still, it is important to have hope. Optimism at age fourteen might result in a very different ending than one for the seven-year-old. The older protagonists might realize that it is up to them to create their own happiness. They might even understand that they cannot always win, but that they define their end result by being resilient and by doing their best. For them, pride in their effort might be a believable happy ending. The very division of forces into good and evil changes as the child matures. In fairytales, good and evil may be totally polarized. There is a good protagonist, and an evil antagonist. But in plays for older children, these forces become progressively internalized, until the time comes when good and evil may be contained within the same individual. As in fine wines, complexity, and a bit of ambiguity, are desirable qualities in plays.

Playwrights for young audiences may consider elements like optimism, the nature of good and evil, and the critical need for ambiguity which can allow the child to form some of his or her own conclusions about the story's meaning. Or they may consider none of these factors and still write well for young audiences. The techniques of writing a play for young audiences are not appreciably different from those of writing a play for adults. A good play still needs a beginning, middle, and end. The climax should be brought about by the needs and intentions of the principal characters. The audience should care what happens to those characters. Of course, a good play also invites meaningful collaboration from actors, designers, directors, etc. One advantage that the TYA writer has is the lack of expectations from child audiences. Because they are more willing than adults to accept any set of conventions that can be coherently and consistently exposed to them, the writer is free to invent styles and theatrical language that adults might balk at accepting. The one caution that I offer to playwrights for the young: you must never, never, never—I think I may stress this point a bit—*never* be condescending. Over simplifying, over clarifying, over stressing text or actions, or talking down to anyone, child or adult, is one sure way to have them dismiss you and your message. Children are, perhaps, tolerant of adults who condescend to them—they need to be as there is far too much of it in their lives, beginning with the well-meaning adults who speak to them in baby talk; but they do not really like it, and they do not usually learn positive messages from those adults.

For many years, as the field of TYA grew in this country from its beginning as a largely social service field into its present form as an arts field, condescension was all too common. Older theatre artists who remember the 1950s and 60s can recount horror stories of theatre for children where the actors shouted their lines, the scenery was brightly colored and uncreative, the characters were one-dimensional, and the moral was clearly stated at the end. For twenty or thirty years after World War II, TYA sprang up in far flung places around America, as well as spawning a dozen touring companies that moved from town to town, often performing overwrought and insincere dramas. True theatre artists learned to shun the concept of children's theatre, and very few respected artists would even consider working in this field. Even the children, who had no other theatrical experience to serve as a base of judgment, could sense that this was an infantile activity of limited amusement. Of course, bad productions still exist for child audiences, but now there are good ones, as well. Things began to change as several factors caused a new look to be taken at young audiences. In the mid-1960s, the regional theatre movement was expanding vigorously. Leaders of that movement saw a need to develop young audiences who would grow up with a proper appreciation for top quality theatre, and become their future audiences. In some cases, these regional theatres began to sponsor some type of TYA, perhaps with junior members of their resident company. University theatre departments also began offering programs and courses in child crama, which often included training a few serious theatre students interested in joining this new field. There were also a few dedicated artists who braved their colleagues' derision by working in the TYA field, and slowly and painstakingly raising its standards. For example, Orlin and Irene Corey's Everyman Players, founded in 1957, did works of stunning beauty that made no compromises in character depth and challenging subject matter. And in Minnesota, where the Guthrie had just opened, John Clark Donahue and his associates developed a TYA company in 1965 known for its poetic scripts and lavish visual productions that has become the Tony-winning Children's Theatre Company of Minneapolis. Other specialist TYA companies of note continued to open or expand across the U.S.A. throughout the 1960s and 70s.

One of the biggest influences on the scripts and productions of this growing field came from overseas. In 1965, the first international conference was held of an organization known as *Association International du Theatre pour l' Enfance et la Jeunesse* (the International Association of Theatre for Children and Young People) (ASSITEJ). This international showcase allowed many American delegates to enjoy their first experience of full-scale professional TYA. Nations like the Soviet Union, Sweden, and the Netherlands were creating excellent productions with nationally prominent artists, and major government funding. In the spring of 1969, I was able to research and complete a doctoral dissertation on principles and practices at twelve selected TYA companies, chosen from both Eastern and Western Europe. Here

119

was none of the condescension or simplification that plagued the developing TYA in America. These were major companies—some with their own resident orchestra and a veritable army of artists and technicians—who were producing excellent theatre for audiences of children starting at age four, in developmental stages up through college age young adults. The scripts they were producing ranged from elaborately mounted fairytales to gritty contemporary dramas. And almost instantly, a complete repertoire of production-tested, age-appropriate scripts were available in this country, provided suitable translations could be made. The infusion of this body of literature acted to 'jump start" American playwriting in the TYA field. With the example of our international colleagues as inspiration, suddenly TYA began to be a credible and even notable profession. American playwrights, like Joanna Kraus and Suzan Zeder, began to be nurtured and produced, and the drive to open serious specialist TYA companies continued. By then, there were even two dedicated publishing houses that sought to disseminate plays for young audiences. New Plays, Inc. published British plays and translations from the Soviet Union, and Anchorage Press brought us the works of Belgian playwright Arthur Fauquez and others. Within a period of less than twenty years, we went from having primarily Charlotte Chorpenning's simplistic and formulaic scripts; to having many choices, by fine writers, of serious targeted plays for young people. In 1989, a consortium of four specialist TYA Companies (Minneapolis, Seattle, Honolulu, and my own company in Louisville) began a project to commission playwrights from the adult theatre to create works for young people. The goal was not only to invite these writers to create works for our audiences, but also to send the message to our adult theatre colleagues that the American TYA had matured, at least in the area of playwrights and scripts.

Of course, there are never enough good scripts. The development of new work continues to be a vital need. As I write this, two national biannual programs operate in alternate years, promoting playwrights and scripts for the TYA. The Bonderman National Youth Theatre Playwriting Symposium, sponsored by Indiana University-Purdue University Indianapolis and the Indiana Repertory Theatre invites direct submissions from playwrights, and the New Visions/New Voices workshop, sponsored by the Kennedy Center in Washington, D.C. invites submissions from theatres committed to a new script. Other TYA companies regularly commission and produce new plays. Many playwrights now cross over between the adult and youth audiences. Translations and co-productions from ASSITEJ partners in other nations also continue to feed into the repertoire.

Playwriting is a very personal act. It is best done in a room by an individual trying to get a vision on paper or on a computer disc. But bringing a play to life is a very collaborative act. It requires a theatre to commit to new work. It requires a director and actors and designers and technicians and, especially, audiences that will buy tickets to new work. While the playwright in a room alone may hold a concept of the play inside his or her mind, it isn't theatre until it reaches the audience's perceptions. And that almost invariably involves rewriting. Exactly as in the adult theatre, creating a play for young audiences is best accomplished when there is true collaboration and trust between the writer and the theatre's production team. Some collaborations profit from the inclusion of a dramaturg on the team—someone who can act as a buffer between the vision of the writer and the immediate needs of the production. In the TYA, it is particularly useful to have someone on the team who is an expert on the needs of the target age group of children. The playwright needs to be a good playwright, but in production, developmental concerns of specific age groups of audiences may be a factor in the play's ultimate success. An educator, a dramaturg, or a director with an awareness of child psychology is a positive asset in the production of new work. This enables the playwright to concentrate on his or her own vision during the writing process, and allows the rewriting process to include shaping the piece for a specific stage or multiple stages in the audience's development.

The storyteller in our ancient village has been replaced, in part, by a theatre troupe—a team of artists working to tell a relevant story. The act of getting the story told has become, in many cases, a business venture, which I shall explore in later essays. But one thing has not changed. It still all starts with a story that needs to be told, and that will create cultural literacy and an awareness of values in its young audience.

12. THE TRANSLATOR

Our minds construct an understanding of the universe around us by piecing together information from many sources, using our senses and different ways of knowing. These bits of information are filtered through our own mental associations, which can also be thought of as our unique perception of reality. Finally, they are synthesized into meaning in our brains, and we develop a particular awareness of the universe, on which we base our thoughts and actions. These bits of information, or clues, enter our minds as sensory stimuli, but often the stimuli are clustered into larger units, which we may perceive as pictures, chronological events, or human behaviors. Take the example of reading a four-panel cartoon strip in the newspaper. First, we have to be able to see the cartoon strip correctly. In our culture we have learned to look at the strip from left to right, so that the four panels form a chronology; there is a sequence, and we understand that the first panel happens before the second, the second before the third, and so forth. Then, we have to perform an aesthetic process on the lines in the first panel. The cartoonist has placed marks on a flat piece of paper, but we perceive these marks as a picture, perhaps of a human female, perhaps talking to a dog. From our past associations, and memory of prior cartoons, we may be aware that the female's name is Cathy, and that the dog is her loyal, but manipulative pet. We also know that the words in the small balloon above her head represent her speech to the dog. In the fanciful style of this cartoon, we are able to read the dog's thoughts in the next panel. The dog chews on Cathy's slipper, and in the next panel Cathy gives the dog a treat, rescuing the slipper. The sequence continues, until a resolution of humor and irony takes place, and we react by recognizing and smiling at the situation. Then we go and give our own dog a treat, in appreciation of its loyalty to us, and perhaps in subtle acknowledgment of the universality of a pet dog's manipulative nature.

In this simple action, we have used many different mental processes. We have recognized a particular form of communication. We have arranged the units in the correct chronological order. We have perceived flat marks as representing pictures of characters. We have interpreted the characters' speech, their emotional states, and even extrapolated their thought processes. We have understood a completed behavior, and we have reacted to it with emotion and a behavioral act of our own.

Psychologists have studied the different ways we have of learning about the world around us, and the different mental activities we use to process that information. From the middle of the 1950s through the early 1980s, much attention was given to a model proposed by J. P. Guilford, who suggested that the structure of intellect could be conceptualized as a cube. (*The Nature of*

Human Intelligence, New York: McGraw-Hill, 1967) One face of the cube contained five mental operations: cognition, memory, divergent production, convergent production, and evaluation; a second face represented increasingly complex products: units, classes, relations, systems, transformations, and implications; and the third face listed five content areas: visual, auditory, symbolic, semantic, and behavioral. Each intersection of the three vectors represented a different mental ability, such as "remembering visual systems". More recently, Howard Gardner has proposed that there were more than five content areas, or as he termed them, intelligences. (*Multiple Intelligences: The Theory in Practice*, NY: Basic Books, 1993) His ideas have gained wide acceptance in education circles, and most schools now advocate some form of instruction and/or measurement of abilities in the areas of *verbal, logical/mathematical, visual/spatial, bodily/kinesthetic, musical, interpersonal, intrapersonal,* and *naturalist* intelligences. In each of these intelligences, the processes of cognition, memory, evaluation, etc. might take place. Individuals have different strengths in different intelligences, and there has been pressure to replace older tests that measured primarily verbal or semantic skills with those that allow for a variety of abilities to be evaluated. Modern teacher education places considerable emphasis on training classroom teachers to maximize student learning by allowing the widest possible range of intelligences to be included in daily instruction and testing.

The implications of this concept in producing a work for the theatre are particularly relevant to the role of the stage director. The playwright has provided the script in a form which is principally verbal, although in stage directions there may be important requirements for visual/spatial or bodily/kinesthetic expressions. But theatre, as an art form, is capable of involving *all* of the human intelligences. The characters speak the text, which is the verbal message provided on the pages of the script. But intrapersonal and interpersonal behaviors occur—human behaviors of both a reflective and an interactive nature; and ought to drive the action of the play. Obviously, there is a continual visual/spatial picturization coming from the scenery, costumes, stage patterns, etc., and frequent bodily/kinesthetic expressions as the characters sit, kneel, move and, perhaps, touch each other. There are symbolic elements, perhaps, among the props or other aspects of the production, and these create multiple logical/mathematical levels of meaning. There may be a musical background going on simultaneously, or the very language chosen by the playwright may give a musicality to the text. Meaning relative to our environment might trigger analysis by the naturalist intelligence. Two additional intelligences have also been theorized: *spiritual* and *existential*. If they are found to be valid, they will also be seen to be contained within realm of the stage production. As the director and the production team send multiple messages to the audience through all of these different channels, the audience's experience of theatre is enriched. One of the great appeals of the theatre is that we, as the audience, do feel as though we are fully engaged. Each of our abilities may inform our experience. Moreover, we may use that intelligence which is our strongest one to compensate for weaknesses we may have in other intelligences, just as we do in life. In a good production, some audience members understand everything they need to know by watching the behavior of the characters, while others are more attuned to subtleties of language and what is being implied by the choice of words.

I would have stage directors consciously be aware of the eight or more channels of intelligence, and take upon themselves the task of insuring that all of these channels are communicating effectively all of the time. Basically, I conceive of the director as a translator. The job is to take the verbal text, provided by the author, and render it into several other languages, simultaneously. It must be translated into pictures, into movement and physical touches, into appropriate symbols, into inner thoughts and sub-text, into human interactions, into musical harmonies or discords, etc. Directors must train themselves to focus on each of these intelligences individually and perceive the play as it would be experienced by a person gifted in that particular intelligence. While directors, like most people, are probably more facile in one type of intelligence than in others, they need to evaluate the production during rehearsals from all of the other modes of knowing as well. To experience the play as one who is predominantly verbal is fairly easy—one may merely cover one's eyes, and focus on what the auditory channels are communicating. To check on the messages being sent in the other modes of knowing is trickier. Can you block your ears and watch a rehearsal in order to follow the play's meaning without its sounds? This eliminates the words, but it also eliminates many other elements––musicality, and the behavioral aspects of language, such as the emotion behind the delivery of lines, or the non-language sounds that humans often make that are enormously expressive.

For many of us, heavily reliant on language to learn and communicate, vocabulary is the aspect of knowing that overwhelms all others. Taking away the play's vocabulary is one of the best ways to evaluate the success of a translation into multiple intelligences. As blindness seems to sharpen the other senses, without vocabulary, all of the other intelligences seem much easier to recognize. Seeing a play in a foreign language that one does not understand, for example, leaves one with all of the relevant cues except for the verbal ones. There is still the musicality of the speech, and all of the interpersonal, intrapersonal, visual, symbolic, etc. information, but no vocabulary. In this condition, it is possible to sense how a play is communicating in ways that exclude its text. I highly recommend that directors train themselves by watching plays in foreign languages. This technique is a stellar training method for all directors, but it is especially helpful to those who will be working for audiences with diminished verbal skills. I believe that there are at least three situations common in today's theatre world, where the audience is likely *not* to be relying principally on their verbal intelligence to grasp the full meaning of the play: an opera in a foreign language, a Shakespearean play in Elizabethan English, and a TYA play where the children are too young to have a fully developed verbal intelligence. For these three audiences it is vital that the director ensure that the play's principal message is being provided in non-verbal channels of knowing.

Seeing a play in a foreign language, of course, trains and sensitizes directors, but it doesn't help them check the effectiveness of a production they may be working on currently. One technique for accomplishing a non-vocabulary test of what an evolving production is communicating is to conduct a rehearsal during which the actors speak exclusively in gibberish. In her book, *Improvisation for the Theatre* (Evanston: Northwestern University Press, 1963), Viola Spolin uses gibberish as a training technique for actors, but it also has application for a director who wants to check a production's communication range. The actors are required to perform the play, as rehearsed, but speaking in nonsense syllables. It is sometimes tricky to get the actors to really speak nonsense. They will often try to make word substitutions, such as trying to convert their lines to "Pig Latin," which will not accomplish the goal of removing vocabulary completely from the rehearsal. But if the actors are coached until they drop the crutch of word substitution, and truly speak in random sounds, the results can be thrilling. On more than one occasion,

I have discovered that the actors, barred from communicating with words, have tripled their energy, directing it into gesture, emotional coloring to their voices, concentration, etc. In fact, I have thought it might be fun to actually perform for an audience in gibberish. As young children are limited in verbal skills anyway, a gibberish—or foreign language—play ought to be appealing to them, if it is projected effectively in every other channel of communication. For most opera audiences, and at least some audience members at a typical Shakespeare production, the actors *are* speaking in gibberish. The point is that a well-directed play should be able to convey meaning without vocabulary, even though the text is the foundation on which the edifice of the production has been constructed.

I am not proposing that the text be literally translated into visual signs. That would be both ponderous, and a wasted opportunity. On the one hand, it is important to remember one limitation of translation, which applies when translating from a verbal mode to a visual or behavioral one, just as it applies when translating from Greek or French into English. No translation is exact. Even the simple English word "please," is rendered as four words in French. *S'il vous plait* literally means "if it pleases you." Any information moved from one channel of intelligence to another will be modified in some way. Some meaning will be lost, and other meaning , possibly misleading, may be gained. On the other hand, this provides the director with an excellent opportunity to *add* texture, and even meaning, to a play. In addition to translating from one channel to another, the director is simultaneously interpreting and embellishing the content of the play. Two productions using the same text may be considerably different from each other, in part because of non-exact choices in how a translation is made. Take for example, Hamlet's well-known, "To be or not to be?" While he says those words, the actor may also be moving or gesturing. The director and the actor can make many possible choices for intrapersonal or bodily/kinesthetic meaning to be overlaid on the verbal text. He may draw out his dagger and stare at it as a means to kill himself. He may search frantically through the book he often reads to find inspiration to carry on with his life. There is literally no limit to the physical messages that could be sent—and all of them partially translate the text, and additionally comment or expand upon it. The same thing can be done by choosing music to add to the production at this moment. An infinite variety of sounds could overlay the performance of the text. In this way, the director creates complex translations of the verbal stimuli, provided by the playwright, into all of the modes of knowing for the audience to absorb, as they choose -- given their own biases and perceptions. If the text represents the original language of the play, the visual, the kinesthetic, the behavioral, the musical, the symbolic, etc., represent the director's translations.

The audience, of course, is free to attend to any aspect of these many offered stimuli that they choose. In a film, or media production, the director has the ability to focus at least the visual field of the audience with precision. The camera unerringly controls what is seen. Now there is a wide shot, and the audience sees the physical relationship between the characters. Now there is a close-up and we see the reaction of the listener. Now there is a tight shot of the hand holding the critical pair of scissors. In the live theatre, the entire field of view is open, from which the audience may choose any object or person on which to focus. There are so many things going on simultaneously on the stage, in so many different modes of knowing. How can we be sure that the audience will be able to follow the story? What causes them to be looking in the right place at the right time so that they see the key touch between characters, or the symbolic prop used for the first time? I have often thought that the primary meaning of the word "director" is the person who *directs the audience's attention*. By carefully constructing stage pictures, the director cues the audience where to look at any given time. By the timing with which gestures, or words, or props, or special lighting effects are introduced, the audience notices various bits of information. The verbal channel, if properly understood by the listeners, should also be telling them what is important in order to follow the story, but all of the other modes of knowing are also bombarding the audience with stimuli. It is up to the director to make sure the right stimulus is perceived at the right time. In addition to being a translator, the director must be an orchestrator, giving focus to the different "instruments" of the theatre at appropriate times.

All of this complexity brings forth another skill of the director. He or she must also be an effective administrator. Different channels or intelligences are being presented by different members of the production team. The actors have the biggest job, of course. They speak the text, embody the kinesthetic action, and reveal intrapersonal and interpersonal behavior. They are also a part of the visual/spatial world we see. But scenery, props, costumes, and lights add much to the visual and often carry symbolic meanings. The sound designer creates the musical channel. As timing is critical to control the audience's attention, all of these elements must work in harmony. From instilling teamwork to creating rehearsal schedules, the director creates an environment for the collaborative work to be done. While there are, no doubt, many personality styles that can effectively mold a production, there are also directors with great visions who fail because they cannot consistently pull together a creative team that is both yielding to a central vision, and productive in their own small part of the totality.

All of the preceding requirements for a director hold true no matter what the age of the audience. To be successful in directing for the TYA, there is really only one additional consideration. Children constitute one of those special audiences that are limited in verbal understanding, as mentioned above, so the skill of translating the text into a visual, behavioral, or other type of language is particularly vital. But the additional consideration of which I speak is really a *willingness* to be directing for young audiences. Many fine directors are not challenged by the task of producing plays for children. They pursue an aesthetic that is more sophisticated, they believe, or that portrays a crueler, more anxious world than that typically shown in TYA material. While there is much in TYA material that can be cruel or anxious, it is also true that optimism, as defined in the last chapter, is very prominent in this literature. If a director wants to portray a pessimistic outlook on life—and that is certainly a valid message for an artist to be portraying; perhaps it is best if that director not try to connect with the young audience.

For me, it has been a great joy to engage that audience, and never has implied a sense that I was excluding important societal concepts, including cruelty or anxiety. While working on my dissertation in 1969, I had the opportunity to interview the distinguished Soviet director, Zinovi Korogodsky, in Leningrad/St. Petersburg. When I asked him for the motive behind his work in this field, he replied, "I want to have a serious talk with the children." Those words have stayed with me. I find myself wanting to talk to the audience, both as a group in the theatre by means of the play itself, and individually afterwards in a face-to-face conversation. I love to watch the audience watching the play. I try to see the play through their eyes. Most of the time, our "serious talk," consists of me directing and them reacting to the work. I want to show them my vision of the world we live in, and help them see a vision of a world that they might make.

When I go into the TYA to direct a play, I want to accomplish all of the goals indicated above. I also want to enjoy myself. I want to effectively translate the text into many modes of knowing, I want to preside over an effective collaborative process, I want to have a serious talk with the audience—perhaps about serious things, or perhaps about humorous or inspirational things. But I also want to stay engaged myself. I love the theatre. I wouldn't be able to work in it unless I did. I direct every play in such a way that it carries a message for me, and every time I watch a rehearsal or performance, I expect to receive that message "for the first time" again. While there is a part of my work that focuses the production on the specific age group for which it has been tailored, there is also a part of me that addresses the production to the so-called 'family" or multi-age audience. There is always a level of meaning that the children will not necessarily get. They live in a world where they do not expect to understand everything. That motivates their search for meaning and growth toward maturity. So including non-intrusive elements that may be above their comprehension is not a barrier to them, but a challenge to continue their development. And those elements help entertain and motivate the adults who bring the children to the theatre. And, perhaps most importantly, they help ensure that I will stay interested in the work that I am doing. I believe it is possible to have a serious talk with the young audience, and also to inspire yourself to creative artistry. If you can do those two things at once, you ought to work in the theatre for young audiences.

13. THE ACTOR/PRIEST

About fifteen thousand years ago, a man crawled into a cave in

ART: THE ACTOR/PRIEST

what is now southern Europe to cast a magic spell. (It could have been a woman, no one really knows, and other men or women crawled into other caves in other places, almost everywhere that the race of humans lived in those glorious Paleolithic days. But let's just follow our hypothetical solitary man for a moment.) He crawled into that cave, perhaps in Lascoux or Altamira, carrying pigments and crude brushes made from sticks or feathers. This man was on a critical mission. His job was to conjure or somehow coax the world around him into providing sustenance for his tribe. If he failed, the weaker members of the tribe would probably starve and die. If he succeeded, much honor would be given to him. Carefully he began to paint a bull on the wall or ceiling of the cave. This image had the magical power to summon the real bulls to the hunting ground. If the painting was authentic; if the man instilled in it the proper magic, the hunters would find and kill a bull, and the tribe would eat. Or, put another way, if the hunters were successful, the cave painting must have been authentic, and therefore the painter must have endowed it with magical powers.

   One principal concept of prehistoric magic is that we control the universe by symbolic mimicry. If I make a doll out of cloth or wood, and place some relic of my enemy on the doll—his fingernails or hair, perhaps—the doll becomes a symbolic replica of my enemy. Then if I stick pins in the doll, and my magic works, my enemy will feel the pains—will mimic the doll's condition. The cave painting is almost the same kind of magic. The artist/magician pairs the symbolic painting of the animal to the real animal by creating a symbolic likeness. That summons the real animal to its fate. In a later period, a dancing shaman replaced the cave painter. If the animal could be successfully mimicked with a mask and the right movements, that would cause the real animal to come forth to the hunters. This magic was obviously critical to the survival of the tribe. If the magic was sloppily done, or the mimicry was ineffective, the animal did not appear to the hunters, and the tribe did not eat. Given the importance of this magic to survival, how did the tribe pick its shaman? If you really believe that your life depends on the effective mimicry of the antelope dancer, by what criteria is the dancer selected?

From our position as twenty-first century scientific thinkers in a sophisticated America, we assume that the dance was probably not the cause of the hunt's success. It must have been luck or chance that decided whether the hunters would make their kill. But that thoughtful position ignores the power of faith as a motivator. If the hunters were convinced by the effectiveness of the dance that they would succeed, might they not have worked a little harder, sought a little longer for their prey? Or contrarily, if they left on the hunt despondent because the dance had not gone well, might they not have been inclined to give up sooner, or search with less enthusiasm, since they knew they were probably going to fail? Human nature being what it is, we tend to make things happen at least partly because we believe that they *will* happen. That dancer who was most able to convince the hunters that they would succeed, was therefore the best dancer—the one most suited to be the shaman. In other words, the one who moved the best, who imitated the antelope the best, who convinced the audience that he was like the antelope, was the one selected by the tribe to be their magician. The *best artist* was chosen to serve the tribe, and they believed in him and his power—which helped to guarantee that his power would work.

Actors have always had the ability to excite their audiences to love or fear. If you believed in the power of the shaman—you would fear arousing his anger. If you believed he could guarantee your survival, you might grow to love or even worship him. For the prehistoric humans, artists were as priests, they interceded with the natural world on our behalf. The origins of art and religion are so closely intertwined, that often they still merge in some inner psychological awareness. The power that the actor has to change into another being is magical and mystical. At times it seems that the actor's body has been overcome and captivated by the spirit of the other creature—the character portrayed. At other times, it may seem that the actor's spirit has enslaved the character's psyche. The notion of one creature overcoming another's being can be a powerful one, inspiring awe and terror. But it is also a spiritual notion, for many worshipers seek to be overcome with the passion of their chosen god, sometimes even using peyote or other drugs, or whirling feverishly to incite the fervor.

This kind of obsession might be perceived as a public threat. Changing into another being, or merging with gods or demons could be seen as dangerous behavior. The Puritans in 17th century England closed all of the theatres for fear that actors' transformations were somehow manifestations of evil. At the very least, their role playing and pretense set bad examples of behavior to their congregations. These are the same Puritans who influenced much of the early immigration into this country. The long neglect of the arts in American public policy is at least partly due to this national heritage of suspicion, a legacy of our founding fathers. A similar pattern is seen wherever theocracy predominates. (Perhaps it is sibling rivalry, Art and Religion practically being litter mates.) Fundamentalists, no matter what their religion, often see art as a strong competition to the beliefs they espouse, are almost universally leery of artists, and often ban them from society. But in more tolerant societies, the arts may become accepted as a corollary activity, not necessarily displacing religion, and artists may achieve a position of honor and celebrity– sometimes far above their actual merit.

In modern society, hunting for antelopes is no longer the principal way by which we insure our survival, and magic is now an amusement, not a necessity. Magic has become an entertainment—a mere exercise in sleight of hand, or technical misdirection of the audience's attention. But the mysterious power to imitate reality, and thereby affect perceptions of the universe is still with us. The antelope dancer has evolved into the performing artist, and the ritual of the pre-hunt dance has become a myriad of entertainments. The live theatre, and especially its sister, media-enabled forms—cinema and television—are ubiquitous in our modern lives. An overwhelming majority of Americans watch television daily and many have come to believe that their favorite characters on their weekly sit-coms or crime dramas are almost real. They discuss soap opera relationships as if they were discussing their neighbors' domestic problems. They probably do not head for the office with the fear that an actor's bad performance on last night's police drama will cause them to be arrested at work, but they do accept certain characters as role models, and mold their own workplace coping techniques around those that their favorite crime-solvers use. And just as they once venerated the shaman, they continue to endow the performer with a respect suggestive of the fact that they still believe he can do magic. Well-known performers can be accorded so much attention that they seem larger than life, and arbiters of taste. They pass from being performers to the level of being celebrities.

Celebrity status in our society comes partly from the exposure that journalists—hungry for news that will attract readers or viewers—give to any familiar face. But there is also a sense of real power that we perceive as belonging to those famous people. It is almost an art form in and of itself. We believe that we perceive a quality in them, a greatness, that is created from stimuli provided by an army of paparazzi, not based in fact. We suspend our disbelief that celebrities are ordinary people and come to accept that they are more important than we are. Artists are not the only group accorded this status in our society, athletes and politicians also attract a disproportionate share of news coverage, but artists are the group that is recognized precisely for their ability to project an alternate persona on the stage or screen. They are famous because they can pretend to be—and make us believe that they are—someone else. We love them, at least partly, because they have shown us the possibility of escaping from ourselves. They can be a different person, live a different life. To the extent that we wish we could escape from our own lives, that power they have is what elevates them to greatness in our eyes. Where we used to worship them because we believed they influenced the success of the hunt for food, now we worship them for their skills at escaping reality. But the passion is the same. They are still perceived with a religious fervor, as a kind of actor/priest.

If adults are swept away with such admiration for public figures, imagine the reaction of children when they come into contact with such magicians. In particular, I am interested in the response of children to adult actors, who are performing in a play at a theatre or in their school. The way the children respond to those actors is much more intense than a casual encounter would suggest. They often respond as if they sensed an enormous power and magical ability in the actors. No one has done any scientific studies to analyze the nature of their responses, but the subject is of great interest to anyone proposing to produce Theatre for Young Audiences. In my experience, children respond to actors, even those they have never met or heard of, with a trust and energy that suggests that of the prehistoric tribesmen for their actor/priests. I hypothesize that there are at least three processes going on that would, collectively, explain this phenomenon.

First, celebrities to the child's mind are not necessarily the same celebrities that adults pursue. Children generally don't read newspapers or fan magazines so they are not impressed by public testimonials. But they are impressed that any adult besides their teachers or family members would spend time and energy on them. That a group of adults would devise a theatre experience for a group of children is perceived as a rare gift from the "big people's world". Nearly all adults who engage children seriously, when they don't have to, are given some celebrity status. I have gone into a second grade classroom as a volunteer to coach three or four individual children with their reading. Obviously, the children I am working with know and respond to me. But all of the other children in the class also treat me like a celebrity. Just by showing up inside the children's world, adults merit special recognition.

Second, there is a perceived comradeship between the children——for whom role playing is still an active form of learning and a daily pastime—and the actors, who are role playing in public and are apparently encouraged to do so. As they grow up, children progress from learning exclusively by imitating behaviors, speech sounds, activities, etc. towards a more complex pattern of learning by reading and absorbing information, listening to instructions, and many other non-participatory forms of acquiring information. But playing out roles is their initial form of access to knowledge, and some form of it lasts well into adolescence, if only via video games. To see adults playing out roles forms an instant bond between the actors and the audience. (Children are fascinated anytime an adult engages in behavior perceived as childlike. If an adult cries or pouts openly, children are truly amazed.)

Third, there is the awe that comes from realizing that these adults are becoming other beings, right in front of the audience. This process is more nearly related to the adult response to an actor. It recognizes the artist's skill at playing in the art form. Perhaps at a level of collective unconsciousness or racial memory, there is an understanding that the better the performance is at imitating a life form, the more likely we are to survive as a tribe. The same passions that infused the antelope dancer, and transported the religious zealot, are happening here before them. They are actual witnesses to actors becoming legendary creatures, characters from familiar tales, or recognizable human beings who remind audiences of their neighbors or friends. Audience members universally seem to admire that power of the actors to transform themselves.

After a typical TYA experience, if the performance has been of a high quality, the acting company will find it has been elevated to a celebrity status in the minds of those children that would be the envy of any press agent trying to promote a new performer. Typically, actors in the field of TYA do not make large salaries, and are not given much peer recognition. But if the adoration of young people is rewarding to them, they will have that in quantity. To the child audience, the actors are performing a vital service, equivalent to that of the cave painters and antelope dancers. If there is respect on both sides, there is almost universally an acceptance by the child of the actor/priest as an intermediary between our world and the world of magic.

14. RIDING THE TIGER, or INSTRUCTIONS FOR THE ACTOR

An actor once told me that acting for children was a little bit like riding a wild tiger. It was a powerful feeling to be up there, but you better make sure you don't fall off! There is certainly an untamed nature to the young audience. Just listen to the cacophony of a school group sitting in their seats before the house lights go down! But once the lights dim, and the play starts, all of that energy is immediately yielded up to the stage, and all the actors have to do is channel it into an amazing aesthetic experience. But how is that done? What harnesses that raw energy, and turns it into an enthusiastic audience response? Is there a difference between acting for children and acting for adults?

When he was asked to explain what was required in order to act for children, Stanislavski is supposed to have said, "It's like acting for adults, only better." In the TYA field, that quote is often heard, but perhaps it does not completely address the questions surrounding a very real issue: "How to act for children?" To start with, I think that by saying "better," Stanislavski was pointing out the critical importance of *integrity*, and *respect* for the audience. Respecting young audiences has to do with treating them seriously—engaging them in that "serious talk" that I mentioned in an earlier essay. At some level, the actors, enjoying that magical relationship with the children described in the last chapter, are influencing the future of the human race. Perhaps Stanislavski was reminding us that giving young people an intense and moving experience in the live performing arts is a serious and important aim? The actors should treat the audience as individuals and as a group with dignity and equality.

Integrity, on the other hand, assumes that the young audience may not be equal to adults—at least in experience and sophistication. Although they are quick to read nuances in emotion and behavior, the audience members may not be practiced in judging quality. They have few examples of theatre to draw on, so they may not know what to expect in terms of an actor's earnest concentration. Adults are sometimes condescending, so the children may assume that the theatre is a place where that happens regularly. Children also like to eat ice cream, even though they know that ice cream is not the only food they need for good nutrition. It is the actors' obligation, then, to protect the children from the actors' own laziness. Precisely because the children may not know the difference yet between what is good theatre and what is not, the actors must absolutely do their very best work to teach them what quality should be. It is easy to work hard if you know you will be punished or found out for being sloppy. It is only the actor's sense of honor, or integrity, that operates to guarantee hard work when negligence may not be instantly revealed.

There is also an ethical issue when playing for children. Their mental and physical healths are in the actors' power. It is relatively easy to get young audiences excited, even boisterous. They can be made to laugh with a bit of slapstick. They can be aroused to real terror with some effective staging helped with sound and lighting. Basically, young audiences can be *manipulated*, and actors have great attraction for them, and therefore great opportunities to manipulate. I feel it is important to use that power to achieve good outcomes, recognizing that what I define as a good outcome may not be what every parent or teacher necessarily would have chosen. In the essay on the *100% Audience*, I discussed the responsibilities incumbent on producers of TYA. The actors also bear the same accountability. They must be good actors, but they also must be caregivers for the young generation, and they must be good role models.

Because young audiences can be manipulated, and because their aesthetic sense is still developing, they may become totally committed to the experience of the play. As they grow from wanting to participate actively in the telling of the story—from playing along with the actors—toward delegating the job of playing to the actor/priests, they may become deeply emotional, and truly identify with the protagonists. At some stages of development, say at age ten, this sharing of an experience outside the world they know is an incredibly satisfying, even life altering experience. But at other ages—say at thirteen—it can be disturbing. Young adolescents, especially males, often do not like to be at the mercy of strong emotions. Feelings may sometimes become overwhelming when fed by raging hormones in their changing bodies, and they may not want to share with their peers that they are experiencing emotions that are potentially out of control. So they deflect those strong emotions and laugh. Or they may try to break the intensity of the moment by making a joke, occasionally loudly, to let their peers know they are still in control, despite evidence to the contrary. The actors playing a passionate scene with total honesty and commitment may hear the laughter or the joke with that part of their consciousness that they reserve to monitor audience responses, and they may find it upsetting. Actors new to TYA might think the play isn't working; that the audience is misbehaving. But the response of the audience is never wrong—they are responding to what they are experiencing in the way that they must. In Chapter Seven, I described a view of aesthetics which states that the play takes place in the individual minds of the members of the audience. In addition to respect and integrity, it would be very helpful to the actor to have some *understanding* of the ways that children respond at different ages. Directors and educators attached to the theatre may provide this understanding, so it does not necessarily have to be information that actors possess when initially hired for the role, but it is critical that they acquire it before performances begin. Otherwise actors may become disheartened, even angry, at an audience that is perceived as being rude, when in fact, it is being moved. The actor needs great concentration to play on—understanding both the defensive laughter of the thirteen year-old boy, and the potential empathy that his nervous response is hiding.

Once they understand this, actors tend to like the sense of power that they have over the young audience. Having played for an audience that is so attentive, so passionately committed to identification with the characters, and so willing to accept whatever set of conventions the production employs, they often comment on how much less satisfying it can be to play for adults, where one is sometimes not quite sure whether the audience is involved in the play, or just being polite. Children, like tigers, are rarely polite. There may be an initial period of a few minutes at the beginning of a play when they are still following instructions from their teachers or parents, but that soon wears off and they are either held by the play or not. If they are involved, there is an energy exchange between the stage and the house that actually seems to be visible. It can be seen in their bodies as they sit in rapt attention, or tense their muscles in sympathy with the characters. If they are not involved, they make no attempt to hide the fact. They will wiggle subtly, then stretch, and then totally lose interest and squirm or begin a conversation with their neighbors. And once the actors lose the audience, it can be hard to get them back. Of course, insincere acting, condescension, or just a poorly written play can lose the audience. But it may happen that an audience is lost for no reason that the actors can control. A teacher with a misplaced sense of discipline may become upset that the children are responding to the play with loud enthusiasm. Perhaps embarrassed that her students are not following classroom protocol, that teacher may intrude upon the play experience by loudly shushing the class. Or an extraneous event may pull them away, such as a child becoming ill, or a group coming into the theatre late.

It is important for actors to be prepared for all types of audience responses, and be comfortable in how they deal with them. When I am directing, I make it part of my job to coach them about audiences, and help them anticipate reactions. Over the many years of my involvement with TYA, I have discovered that there is one essential piece of advice that actors need to hear, and hear repeatedly, before they begin to play for young audiences. It a simple concept, but one that cannot be taken for granted. It is, perhaps, stated most succinctly by Arthur Miller in *The Crucible*:

> REBECCA NURSE: A child's spirit is like a child, you can never catch it by running after it; you must stand still, and for love it will soon itself come back.

I like to tell the actors to *lean back*. In much of the worst sort of TYA, one sees the audience slip into the early stages of non-involvement, generally known as the "wiggle stage." The actors respond by getting louder, more physical, using bigger gestures, and projecting less sincerity. The audience feels like they are being pushed away, and they go further away. Chasing after the audience I equate to leaning forward and it does not work! Never chase the audience, but rather, as Goody Nurse advises, stand still and let them come to you. The correct response to the first sign of wiggles is to pull the action in towards yourself as a performer. You must become quieter, more sincere, and more vested in your belief in the truth of the acting choice that you have made for that moment in the play. While still audible, the lines must be actively listened to, if they are to be heard. It should almost be like the actor has a secret, and is not sure that he wants to share it. The actor holds that secret firmly in his inner being and protects it from the outside world. That is what I mean by "leaning back." To learn that secret, the audience, if they were ever drifting, must become involved again. And, if the action as written is believable, and the actor's choice is viable, the audience will for love itself come back. Even before the audience starts to wiggle, it is always good to invite them to come toward the play, rather than thrusting it into their consciousness. If forced to distill all I have learned about acting for TYA over the past forty years into one principle, it would be this: "Lean back!"

Occasionally, audiences drift because the action of the play is unwinding too slowly. This might be because the script is over written, it might be because the director has imposed too many interpretations for the plot to bear, or it might be simply because the actor is being over indulgent and wallowing in the emotions of the moment. Whatever the reason, the result is that the audience feels like they have gotten ahead of the play. They already know what is being belabored on the stage; they are ready for the next thing to happen. This problem can be dealt with easily: make it happen faster. Leave out a superfluous acting moment, even if it feels right to the actors. Trim a complex bit of blocking. Or even cut some lines. (I can't believe that I, a sometimes playwright, just wrote that.) If they are losing interest, perhaps it is because there is something in the play that they find repetitious and unnecessary.

At the other end of the continuum, it is possible that the audience is getting lost because the play has skipped a critical moment or transition. The audience feels like they have missed something, and they have now fallen behind the play. This problem is harder to fix, because you first must figure out what is missing, and then you have to add it. The actors and the director have assumed that something was clear because they know it well, having studied the whole play many times. But it is not clear to the audience, experiencing it in real time, and for the first time. The audience is giving you a clue by showing you the exact moment when they get lost. If at two consecutive performances, audiences begin to wiggle at the same moment, you can be sure there is a problem in the script, direction, or acting at that moment in the play. Examine the sequence of conflicts in the scene, review the character's subtext, and try to figure out what assumption the performers are making that is not being communicated to the audience. If the script has been produced before, it is logical to assume that the problem is in the acting or directing. If it is a new play, it may be a missing moment in the text. Experiment by clarifying or adding transitions. The audience will tell you when you fix the problem.

In the essay on Participation Theatre, I also talked about techniques that the actor should know when performing in that particular style. To recap the key points, I emphasized dealing with the actual moments of participation. If audiences are slow to participate, it is usually because they do not believe their help is really needed, or possibly because they are shy about starting out, and just need a clear signal when to begin, such as "on the count of three." If audiences are overly involved, and participating to excess, they can be quieted briefly by introducing a new physical action, but I also stressed the importance of actors understanding the structure of the play so they can quickly proceed to the next new beat, skipping through things that the audience already knows, and presenting the next significant conflict.

Of all the issues actors have raised over the years, the second most common question (after "How do you act for children?") has been, "What do you look for when casting a TYA play?" My bias, of course, is not to cast a single play, but to cast a company. Since I am a great believer in a resident acting ensemble, at Stage One we tried never to cast an actor for just one show. If we did need an extra person for one play, we often would try to bring back a veteran of the company who had gone on to other challenges, but had a current schedule that was compatible with our needs. Failing that, we would look for a newcomer that we were hoping to work into the company in subsequent seasons. One basic reason for the ensemble approach—besides my feeling that it nurtures actors, unlike the predominant casting system in America which merely exploits actors—is that I wanted to make sure that the actors we hired really wanted to do the kind of work we did. Many fine actors will not or can not act for children. The pay is low; the fame may be intense but it is mostly in the minds and hearts of young admirers; the season is long; and our location, Louisville, Kentucky, is in a very livable city that is not exactly a theatre Mecca. On the other hand, the work is steady; the range of roles enormous—from Romeo to a talking tree; the mission is critical—building young hearts and minds, and creating an audience of the future, and the opportunity to grow as an actor is tangible.

The qualities I am looking for in an actor, therefore, must include a commitment to, or at least a willingness to learn about, young audiences. An actor may have been exposed to some bad TYA productions, and have doubts about doing this kind of work, but if they are willing to learn about effective, high quality TYA, they may be welcome. There is also my bias toward ensemble acting and resident companies. I like actors who will fit into a team, and not need to be the star. Actors in our company may play a leading role in one play, and a supporting role in the next one. I have to sense that that would be exciting for them to be in an ensemble and feed off the energy that comes from working with the same team over a period of time. Good company members are also usually interested in other people; they want to see their teammates succeed as much as they want to succeed themselves. That quality is hard to judge in an audition, but I always try to sense its presence, or rely on recommendations from past directors or teachers.

Because of the wide range of repertoire, from Shakespeare for the older student audiences to fairy tales and Participation Plays for the youngest, a lot of different skills are needed. Actors must be able to move well: they may have to play an animal or a goblin. They may have to sing and dance, or even juggle. They should be able to handle a realistic drama, like *The Diary of Anne Frank*, and a presentational style, like *commedia dell'arte* or a broad farce. Obviously, they must have good technical skill—voice, body, and imagination. I like them to be organic, to be able to use their whole bodies to seamlessly become a character, not merely indicating one from the neck up. And, perhaps most critically, I have to believe them; they must project honesty. The good news is that there are actors who can be all of those things. The actors are the core of any theatre company, and it has been my good fortune to work with many excellent and dedicated ones over the years.

Before leaving the arena of thoughts for prospective actors in the TYA field, there is one final point to be made. In my mind, there is a critical difference between an *actor* who is skilled in the craft of acting, and an *artist*, who is skilled in the craft of acting but also has a world view that informs and shapes all of the work. American actors tend to be perceived, perhaps, as "types" or, even less flatteringly, as "packages." One of the worst features of the American theatre as it is commonly practiced is that it feeds off of the idea that actors are narrowly definable. Casting directors will hold auditions, and actors will come in large numbers. Both sides know that the actor who best fits the predetermined image that is in the casting director's head, transferred there in precise detail from the stage director's head, will be the one chosen. This practice assumes that there is only one way to play the role, and that it has already been decided. Casting typically functions to guarantee that the director's vision will be realized. Early in my professional career, I was an observer at an audition where a wonderful actor actually was told by a director that he could not be used because his beard was too long. It would never have occurred to this director to ask the actor to trim his beard because outside in the audition line there would certainly be an actor who could do the same things that this actor could do, but who had a shorter beard. (I am not making this up; it really happened.) Under this system, actors become commodities. Directors buy the exact merchandise that is required, use it, and then discard it. The actor's life then becomes a series of eight-week jobs (three for rehearsal, and five for performance), separated by long periods of searching for work—searching for the spot where they, as a commodity, can fit in exactly. As a producer and director, I rejected this exploitive system long ago.

When I am casting, I am always looking for artists, and I will hire them precisely because I do not know exactly what outcome will result from our period of collaboration on the role. An artist claims the right to be unique. No two of them will play the role the same way, because they will be supporting their interpretation of the text with their own sense of vocation. The words may be the same, but they will not be supported by a generic analysis that assumes there is one right answer, and that the director knows what it is. The actor/artist also has something important to communicate to the audience about the character. The director may understand the script, and know with some precision WHAT happens in the play. This is the external manifestation of the text, and it may be the director's job to clarify this WHAT for the actors and the audience. But the internal life of the characters— the WHY and the HOW of the play—comes from the actors, and the more they are able to bring their own unique sense of why and how the world functions, the more alive the production will be with their message to the young audience. Within the text lies not one truth, but many truths. Only this particular artist will play out this particular truth in this particular manner. Some other artist in the role would find a different set of truths to play. This approach makes actors more than a commodity. They become collaborative artists, contributing their world view to the aesthetic of the play.

The greatest ambition of my life in the theatre has been to put great actors—actors who were also artists—actors who were willing to take the risk of mounting that tiger—in the same room with young audiences, and let the magic interchange happen. Of course, the "magic" never happens without hard work and preparation, but, believe me, it can happen. And when it does, the power of art to change lives is manifest.

15. PICTURES AND SOUNDS

Designing for the theatre for young audiences may be the best kind of designing there is because each time you create designs for a play you are inventing a new Universe, with its own set of rules. In the adult theatre, if a designer chooses to alter reality in the visual elements of a production, even slightly, the audience is suspicious. They instantly notice that the play does not look like the real world. They want to understand the message; they want to know what it *means* if all the costumes are black and white, or if the animal masks have only one ear. Their intellectual instincts are aroused and challenged, and they can rarely just *experience* the fresh new reality of the designer's imagination, but they have to poke at it intellectually until it may even interfere with their enjoyment of the performance.

The young audience is much more trusting. They invariably assume that, being children, they do not understand everything yet. Therefore, whatever is there is what is supposed to be there. They do not hesitate to accept the fact that in this particular world everything is black and white, and in this other world animals have one ear instead of two. This information never interferes with their interest in the story being told, although it may signal them that the world being shown is not the one that they normally live in. They accept the fact that the adults who are showing them this other world are doing so for a reason. It is not necessary to understand the reason; it is only necessary to enjoy the play. In this way, the design concept affects them at an experiential level, instead of at an intellectual one. This makes them an ideal audience for the creative designer, who is able to communicate images directly to the heart, instead of having to negotiate the pathways through the brain. It also removes any necessity for realism or naturalism from the visual world of the play.

Much of the entertainment young people watch is not set in the real world. Consider cartoons and puppets. Both represent life forms that may behave like people in certain regards, but are not subject to the consequences that affect real people. Children are exposed to a lot of cartoons and puppets. In fact, many of those who provide entertainment for very young children seem to assume that only cartoons and puppets are suitable images to present. Cartoons and puppets are clearly not like we are: Wiley Coyote can stop in mid-air and contemplate his impending fall into the canyon. We can see the expression on his face as the dynamite is about to explode. He can die and come back to life again, perhaps several times, in a ten-minute cartoon. Puppets can move their bodies in impossible ways, turning their heads through 360 degrees, or stretching out their necks like a telescope. Cartoon and puppet programs for adults exist, as well, and one of their appeals is that the adults will, in these media, embrace, with childlike understanding, that the unreal can be material for artistic exploration. But children are always in that state.

Illustrators of children's books have long taken advantage of the child's willingness to accept a wide range of creative images as legitimate. If you will look at the Caldecott Award winners, given annually to the best illustrations in a book for young readers, you will see an enormous variety in media and style, but almost no realism. The artist is free to design a world that expresses his or her own creative energy and, ideally, one that also ties into the theme of the book. A vast range of ethnic artistic styles, of colors and shapes, of fragmentary and detailed drawing techniques, are all acceptable. The best choice also brings the particular story into focus. Similarly, theatre designers in the TYA have wide latitude in which to express the visual world of the play, providing only that they also serve the needs of the play.

The needs of the play are, ideally, established between the director and the designers in a collaborative way. Occasionally, when I am directing, I will have a strong visual image of the world I want to share with the audience. But more often, I am trying to communicate a concept of the play, and I trust in the designers to provide the specific images. Unless the recognition of reality is a particular need of the play—and it rarely is in the TYA repertoire—I want them to be bold. I prefer that they create a visual and auditory world that is clearly not this world. And I want the differences to be those that highlight the theme, or action of the particular play. I am a believer in the notion that every play carries its own unique style, although certainly there are clusters of plays that tend towards general categories of styles. Realistic plays group towards one slice of a spectrum, and fantasy towards a different portion, but within those loose categories, each play should look different, and each production of the same play should look different.

This discussion, by the way, ought to be independent of the

ART: PICTURES AND SOUNDS

influence of any budgetary considerations. Some production budgets are large, some are small. I have found a value in both extremes. If a budget is large, the director and designers may fully realize their visions. There may be sound composed especially to accompany the play. The stage pictures may be lavish and create amazement in the young audience. This scale teaches the children that the adult world values them and makes a present to them of this spectacle. It shows an imaginary world with limits removed. On the other hand, if a budget is small, the creativity of the artists may have to substitute for money, and the pictures and sounds may be less imposing and less elaborate. But a spare style encourages the audience to use their imaginations more. It shares with them some of the responsibility for realizing the stage pictures. Instead of a full orchestra, a guitar may be the musical accompaniment. But the actors can sing to a guitar with great effect, and they can easily convince the audience that what they say they see is really there. The children's pictures drawn after such a performance will invariably include visual elements that were believed by the actors but never seen. I have always felt that it was better to expose young audiences to both extremes of production values, rather than to try to do each play on a tight budget. Better one lavish production and four imaginative ones in a season, than a succession of plays offering some partially realized elements of spectacle, but none fully accomplishing the vision, and none really allowing the children's creative imagination to supplement solid but limited choices. In any case, there must be scenery, costumes, props, lights, and sound. (The absence of one of these elements is itself a design choice.) And these design elements must serve the play and add to it all the design richness that assets allow.

Obviously, each play does have specific needs that must be met by the designer. These may be *narrative* needs—Hedda Gabler burns a manuscript, so there has to be a fireplace or stove somewhere on the set; or they may be *psychological* needs—Anne Frank and her family are trapped in a secret annex so there must be a feeling of isolation or captivity about their environment. Sets, lights, sounds, and costumes all reveal information about the people and their surroundings, and this information may be plot revealing as well as mood setting. The lighting or the tolling of a bell may tell us the time of day; the costumes may tell us the profession of the characters; the sets may tell us how wealthy they are. There is also the issue of utilization. The director will move the actors about on the set and make stage pictures that are revealing of plot and feelings. There must be a floor plan, levels, opportunities for sitting, etc. that accommodates both picturization and variety. The costumes must be suitable for the actors' usage, enabling the appropriate kinds of movements, and/or placing the right restrictions on other kinds of movements. The lighting must enable visibility, and add to the picturization of particular moments in the script, but also evolve through time in a way that is unobtrusive, but emotionally satisfying. The sound must add meaning and not confuse us. If there are songs, the music must be audible but not obscure the lyrics. All of these concerns are part of serving the play.

But beyond that service, there is creative design. There are visual elements that communicate directly to the visual/spatial or bodily/kinesthetic intelligence of the audience and that add enrichment and texture to the experience of the play. They may even contradict the information being received from the text or acting. If a designer were, for example, to set *The Diary of Anne Frank* in a space *without* barriers to the outside world, or without separate areas within the annex, perhaps that would be sending a message that the barriers were only in their minds. That may contradict the sense of the text, but it may be done for a reason if the director and designers think it justified. More often, the production elements support the text, but offer an elaboration or an applied sense of it. To follow the same example, what if *Anne Frank* took place in a world of images from other countries and times—from Ireland, or Bosnia, or Rwanda, or any other place where people have been persecuted for being different? That might be adding the textural message that hatred and bigotry are, unfortunately, universal.

It is important to stress that information, received by the audience in the visual/spatial, or bodily/kinesthetic channels, is coming in *simultaneously* with information (i.e. the text) through the verbal channels; plus, if there is music or sound accompanying the action, through the musical channel. (See Chapter 12 for a wider discussion of multiple intelligences.) Therefore, the multiple messages may be supporting or reinforcing each other, or they may be evoking slightly different connotations. The choices available to a team of director and designers with the resources to truly collaborate on the moment-to-moment storyboard presentation of the play are endless.

Of all of the channels in which the audience receives information, the one *least* decipherable to the young child is probably the verbal channel. Clearly, in the adult theatre, the design elements are important to the over-all experience of the play, but in the TYA, the design elements may even *become* the play, with the text only there as a guide to the designers. I have seen productions that were so elaborate and so visually stunning that the pictures easily dominated the text. Although there may be a tendency to dismiss this type of production as "eye candy," or empty of substance, to the child audience—especially those aged eight or below—these kinds of experiences are every bit as valid, and much more accessible, than the more verbal experience of a production dependent on dialogue for its effect. If you will interview a child after such a fully produced performance, you will generally find that they are able to describe the entire production in great detail including the colors on the various parts of the set, the details of the costumes, etc. They are less observant about lighting, but then, so are adults who tend to notice it only when it is wrong. Young audiences may or may not remember much about what was said, but they can tell you what it looked like. As the children grow older, verbal information becomes more and more important to them, but they still retain a strong memory of visual images well into early adolescence. By adulthood, few of us retain the ability to remember vivid details of a visual image long after viewing it. Those few become detectives or decorators, and make good use of that primitive ability to memorize visual images. Most of us lose this skill, and learn to examine the world around us primarily through the verbal channel. But children tend to believe what they see much more than what they hear.

It is therefore obligatory for the TYA practitioner to give young audiences rich, complex, and meaningful visual images. It is a myth that children prefer simple lines and bright colors. That may be true (and it may not be) of infants, who are still learning to process information from their senses. But by the time children are four or five, and attending their first TYA production, they are soaking in information from the visual world. Once again, if you will study the Caldecott winners over the last fifty years you will find very little that would rightfully be called simplicity. Complexity, artistry, and originality are generally what that award commemorates. I would prefer that the young audience be presented with pictures and sounds that serve the play, but also fascinate the mind. They should stand on their own as art works. A single costume or a view of the scenery lit by a particular lighting scheme should, by itself, tell us something relevant to the world of the play. In discussing fine wines, connoisseurs pursue an ideal of *terroir,* by which they mean a kind of uniqueness—a sense of the very place on earth on which those particular grapes were grown. In just such a way, the designs of a play should reflect the very individuality of that particular play. Wine experts can tell at a taste where a great wine comes from. It is good theatre design if a knowledgeable theatre producer can look at a picture and know instantly what play it represents. And it is great design if it represents that play in a way that is both inspirational and unique.

THE BUSINESS OF THEATRE FOR YOUNG AUDIENCES

THE BUSINESS OF THEATRE FOR YOUNG AUDIENCES

16. THE CHARIOT DRIVER

For twenty-five years (1978-2003), I served as the Producing Director of Stage One: The Louisville Children's Theatre, and for many of those years I wore the dual hats of artistic and managing director. Prior to that, I had been artistic director of TYA companies in Florida and New York for an additional eight years. So for thirty-three years I had the opportunity to lead talented and dedicated artists, educators, and administrators in the task of making theatre for young audiences and their parents and teachers. It has been a rewarding and satisfying career, but there were certainly times when it felt that my hardest job was simply to get everyone involved to agree on what the priorities were. Eventually, I developed an image of myself as a chariot driver.

If you want to win chariot races, you have to have strong, fast horses. The trick is to get all of the horses, many of whom possess temperamental natures and sturdy egos, to pull the chariot *together*. They will have a tendency to want to run off on their own, in various directions. Somehow, you have to make them want to work as a team. You must never break the spirit of these champions, or they will lose interest in winning the race. You must never insist on substituting your judgment for their own integrity, although you absolutely have to convince them all to agree to run in the direction you are pointing. Much of your concern between races goes to making sure that all of the horses are well-fed and exercised and rested. On race day, you set the pace of the race as the driver, but you aren't the one who runs; and it is best, I think, to let the horses know that they are the winners, not you.

As there is not one style in training horses, there is also not one style in leading a theatre organization. Each Artistic Director has to find a method that suits his or her own personality. The skills involved in being the boss of an organization are complex, and have been analyzed and explored in hundreds of business courses, and thousands of books on management. Many of those books also draw a distinction between the notion of being a *boss* and the alternate concept of being a *leader*, and, indeed, in most theatre organizations, the two functions are not always synonymous. My preferred role was to inspire a staff with a strong vision, to offer measured steps toward that vision, and to set a personal example of dedication and integrity in working for that vision. But I have seen other highly successful directors work in other ways, and achieve exemplary results.

Complicating the director's role is the tradition in the American professional theatre of a three-headed leadership model. Although many variations exist, the norm is to find a theatre that has an artistic leader, usually called the artistic director; an administrative leader, often titled managing director; and a governing committee of lay citizens operating as a board of directors or trustees. The board is the legal entity that operates a non-profit theatre in the public interest, for which it receives tax benefits, eligibility for grants, etc. The managing director guides the day-to-day operations of the business side, including marketing, sales, fundraising, office and facility management, human resources, etc. The artistic director is in charge of programming, hiring actors, directors, designers, choosing the plays, quality control, etc. These three forces should be in harmony. The artistic director should lead in setting a vision, the manager in implementing an efficient organization to achieve that vision, and the board in insuring that the vision is right for the community, in communicating it to the power structure, and in opening doors for funding and public support. We have all known theatres where one or more of these three elements ended up being perceived in an adversarial role to the others. This can be a very unhealthy situation, and usually ends in a change of personnel, or even in the demise of the theatre program.

In my own history, I was sometimes required to act as both manager and artist, and it was usually not an ideal situation for the theatre when this occurred. The artist is required to dream without too many limits on what is possible, and the administrator is required to measure out what is attainable in the pursuit of those dreams. Trying to do both at once requires a difficult division of purpose. In my own case, I often found that I would pre-censor my own artistic flights, knowing with my administrative side that they would likely strain the theatre's resources. Eventually, I came up with a partial solution by assigning the task of "dreaming" to an associate artistic director, but I felt that Stage One grew most successfully during those periods when we were fortunate enough to have a separate, talented manager. If a dynamic balance can be achieved between desire and ability, everyone involved in the organization senses a positive energy, and in this state arts organizations prosper—growing in a measured way; never feeling desperate, but always moving forward.

Out of my feelings of inner conflict, and a strong need to examine how I could best prioritize the different functions required of me – nurturing a staff of creative egos, balancing artistic ambitions with practical reality, and best serving our dual audiences of public families and school field trips – I developed (in 1996) a personal document that served me very well. Here is the document in its entirety, followed by a paragraph by paragraph expanded discussion:

WHO DO I WORK FOR?
My Seven Masters (in the order served):

1. ***The children in the audience.*** *The children come into the theatre, whether knowingly or not, in search of an aesthetic experience – a moment of identification and caring, of strong emotionality, or a new understanding, or joy or grief. My job is to provide that experience at the appropriate age level.*

2. ***The children not in the audience.*** *How can I get them to the theatre next time? How can I make this theatre and the field of TYA stronger so that there will be many more opportunities for such an experience to reach them?*

3. ***The artists who connect me to the children.*** *They work here, knowingly or not, not just for wages, but because they can magically reach into the children's lives. I do not touch the children directly, but through the funnel of their talent. In return I must work to keep them growing as artists, pushing their own boundaries back with each new assignment, and discovering how to take rewards from their special work. These people are not actors, designers, playwrights—they are artists—who are changing the world around them. I am their leader, guardian, facilitator, big brother, friend, and sometimes, conscience.*

4. ***Myself as an artist.*** *I have to take care of my own needs in the same way. I need to continue to grow new artistic muscles, and to continue exercising the ones I have. I need to effect change; to create concern.*

5. ***The teachers and parents who bring their children to the theatre, knowingly or not, in search of a magical***

experience. *They have the right and duty to make judgments about their children's lives. I am here to assist them in reaching those goals I can assist with, to open up their minds to new possibilities if they are so inclined, and to allow them to opt out of those experiences they do not wish for their children.*

6. ***The community sponsors.*** *They support the work of the theatre for their own valid reasons. It is my job to understand those reasons and work within their expectations, even in those cases when I am trying to refine and educate those expectations. The board of directors has a legal and ethical responsibility to operate the theatre as trustees for the community at large. I am here to help them do it.*

7. ***Anyone else who wants to be my master.*** *The theatre exists as a public institution. Anyone can have a valid (for them) claim on our mission. I do not owe these people any service which might contradict my duties to my first six masters—but I do owe them attention and respect to the same degree that they offer attention and respect to me.*

These seven masters must all be served, to the extent that it is possible with the resources available. But they are ranked very carefully in order. A major part of my job as producing director, as leader of the organization, is to ensure that the priorities are maintained. However, I strongly believe that this prioritizing should remain an internal document reflecting the dedication of energies, and not published to the world at large. No one wants to be told that they are fifth or sixth on the list in importance. I made the mistake once of showing this personal statement of "masters served" to a fundraising consultant, and he was horrified— —by the ordering, if not by the very fact that such a clandestine document existed. How dared I place the Board and community sponsors in the next to the last place, he wondered. But I believe the order to be correct. Each of these masters' needs can be met, and without diminishing the needs of any group higher on the list, if the producing director can manage people in a positive way, and point out to them, when necessary, how serving a higher ranked group is exactly the pathway to meeting their own objectives for the theatre.

For me, the audience comes first. My primary duty is to serve them. It may be the critical defining difference between the TYA and the mainstream regional theatre for adults. The theatres for adults want to have audiences, but they often put the first priority on making art—art that is meaningful to them as artists. Then they hope to find or build an audience for that art. Perhaps this is the correct approach for an adult theatre. But in the TYA, the audience should be the primary purpose for making the art—and then, once their needs are met, we can endeavor to make sure that the art is meaningful to ourselves as well. Ideally, the latter goal helps to achieve the former one, but the priority must always be clear. We have been entrusted with the youth of our community. We must do nothing in the name of art to jeopardize the physical or mental well-being of those young people. Rather we must strive to understand and meet their needs with the highest quality art that we can devise. For each child, a trip to the theatre must be entertaining and emotionally satisfying. We are working to build an audience for the American Theatre, but we are also working to enable each individual child to reach his or her fullest potential as an arts consumer and as a human being.

I have placed the children not in the audience in the second highest position. Of course, it is not their fault that they are not at the theatre; it is because some adult has failed to see the wisdom of bringing them. Often, it is an accident of geography, as one school brings its children to all the plays, and another school a mile away does not. It is unacceptable to me that any child should miss out on the wonder of live theatre because of such a trivial reason. Behind all of the marketing, fundraising, proselytizing, community relations, public promotions, friend-building, and general efforts to create a sense of *need* in the adults responsible for those children, is this principle: *Every child should have access to the arts.* After making sure the current audience is well served, the second priority goes to scheming ways to get more children in to share in the experience. I also include scheming ways to get more theatres to take TYA seriously, and offer more performances. Part of increasing the audience has to be increasing the opportunities to become an audience. Supporting the overall field of TYA, building bridges with the adult theatres that might offer meaningful programs for young people, and raising public awareness of the power of good TYA in the lives of their children is part of this element.

The third group should be obvious—without the artists there can be no art. But simply hiring them is not enough; they also have to be trained, inspired, nurtured, given opportunities to grow, and, when the time comes, pushed out to try their wings in other artistic universes. Many of them have come to work at a theatre like Stage One with the idea that it was a job. They may have reservations about doing something called "Children's Theatre." They may want to get an Equity card, or qualify for health insurance, or just earn a little money to pay off school loans. Most of the time, they are surprised when they find themselves immersed in a passionate company of dedicated artists. Quite often they become inspired by the power and energy and love offered them by the young audience members. Slowly, they discover the range of artistic opportunities available in the repertoire—everything from fairy tales to Shakespeare to realistic modern dramas. Eventually, they grow to understand the nature of ensemble creation, and glory in the relationships they build up with the other artists of the company over many years of growth and effort. It is essential for the leader to guide this process, to offer new challenges that will stretch the artists just as they are becoming complacent, and also to minimize the inevitable personality frictions that can materialize when strong egos work together over many projects. This group of my masters is the one I tend to work with on a daily basis, so their needs can crowd out the needs of the others if allowed. But they are essential to the success of the mission as they are the ones though whom the audience is touched and changed.

Fourth on the list are my own needs. It would be easy to forget to monitor my own growth as an artist or need for satisfaction in my work, but doing so would slowly cause the work to become fatiguing and flat. When creative people forget to nurture their own creativity the result is often "burnout". In addition to giving reinforcement steadily to others, every once in a while you need to receive reinforcement for your own creative work. Of course, I have also known situations where artistic leaders have put this master first among those to be served. That may work well for certain personality types. As an audience member myself, I am often amazed and inspired at the work of a dominant auteur, who shapes a theatrical presentation out of his own genius, pulling fellow artists and audience members along in the energy surge from the stage. But such are not my gifts and I choose to explore my own talents in perspective, relying on surrounding myself with others whose creativity helps to support my own. Nevertheless, it is not wise to ignore your self and your own needs. That temperament may serve in certain professions, but not that of the artistic director, who, after all, is hired to maintain a personal standard of taste and excellence, and promote it as viable for the audience to share.

   The next group is also critical to the success of the mission, for they are the ones who make possible the experience of theatre for their children. A tiny percentage of adults who bring children to a theatre experience may see the theatre as a kind of babysitter––occupying the children for an hour while they run an errand or make some phone calls; but I believe that the vast majority are doing so because they think it will do something positive for the child, either as an art event or as an educational one, or both. Many also hope that they will enjoy sharing a special event with their child or group of children. It has always helped me to assume that most of these enabling adults are my partners in the aesthetic development of the children, and many of them become active partners—enthusiastically choosing the right experiences for their children, carefully following the theatre educators' suggestions for maximizing the experience, and regularly using preparatory and follow-up materials to enhance or build upon the theatre event. I can best serve this group by giving them accurate information so that they may make informed decisions about their choices for the children they protect. Because the theatre is always about something—people in a particular kind of trouble—parents and teachers should know ahead of time what the nature of that trouble is going to be. They have the right to avoid themes and stories that conflict with the values they are trying to teach their children or (at the very least) to prepare themselves to answer children's concerns if important issues are raised by the play they have just seen. Of course, they also should expect a high quality of theatrical experience when they do choose to come and bring their children. I am a parent myself, and that has helped immeasurably in understanding the concerns parents and teachers might have. It is also useful to remember that most of these adults had little or no theatre experience themselves as children. They are giving something to their children that they probably never had themselves, and that is an effort worthy of my support.

The sixth group would possibly come first if TYA was a profit making venture. The sponsors, community leaders, and board members who provide or find the resources to operate the theatre are technically my employers. But as is the case in many not-for-profit ventures, they are the volunteers and I am the professional. Ironically, it is often my job to teach them what to expect from me. One important thing for them to learn: the theatre is not a for-profit business, although it may be important to run it in an efficient business-like way. Non-profits are operated to serve some public need; that is why these volunteers serve (many of them for years) with incredible generosity and serious devotion. In my view, the TYA is a gift that the community leaders give to their children. As producing director, they have entrusted me with the responsibility to suggest appropriate details for the gift, to package it appropriately, and to deliver it. I consider myself most successful at serving this group when I make efficient use of the resources they have provided, and they have a true understanding of why I made the choices I have made, so as to maximize the effect of their gift upon the recipients—their children.

The final group, the general public at large, invites concern from time to time precisely because the theatre is a publicly funded operation. Observers with their own particular interests occasionally come forward to question the subject matter of a play, or the size of a budget. In the long run, it is better to address their concerns honestly and completely. Doing so reinforces the fact that the theatre is a gift to the children, and one in which all adult citizens should share ownership. Dealing courteously with non-involved parties is the best way to get them to be involved. If nothing else it is a chance to open doors that may allow someone from group two above to join group one.

Among the many masters whom I serve, carefully outlined above, I have not included the theatre's administrative staff. To the extent that they are employees, of course, their needs become my concern as boss or leader of the organization. Their skills are very crucial to building the business aspects of the theatre's operation, and they can be instrumental in the theatre's success. Without effective marketing, fundraising, and administration even the best artistic product will struggle to survive. Nevertheless, I did not include them on a list of "masters that I serve," as I always thought of them as partners rather than masters. We worked together to ensure the theatre's survival, but it would be a mistake, I think, to let the theatre's mission be pulled in a direction that might be dictated by administrative needs. Perhaps this is an underlying weakness in my understanding of the theatre for young audiences, and, if so, I freely confess it. My goal has always been to bring joy and enlightenment to the audience – above all else. To reach that goal —to win the chariot race—brings a satisfaction well beyond that of most professions.

17. TWO AUDIENCES

Central to the operation of a successful theatre for young audiences is deciding which population to serve: the public, the schools, or both. Choosing a target audience will affect both artistic and business decisions throughout the organization. The titles chosen for productions to serve teachers and school groups will not necessarily be the titles one would choose to attract parents and grandparents who would bring their families to the theatre. Even the times of day when one performs, and the kind of parking facilities required will be very different if one is expecting school busses filled with fifth graders, as opposed to family sedans with siblings spread out over several ages, their parents, and other members of an extended family. Boards of directors and key staff members need to carefully examine their mission before committing to one of these audiences, or, in those cases where the mission and the resources permit, attempting to serve them both.

By serving school audiences, theatres are addressing 100% of the children who go to school. No child is denied the opportunity for a theatre experience because of lack of parental interest in the arts or family economic status. Free or reduced price tickets are almost always offered to school children who are unable to pay. But school time performances are often perceived as part of the academic day, and not as arts experiences separate and above the normal school offerings. Teachers, in fact, are motivated to make the theatre experience seem to be closely related to the educational life of the school. Also, *choice* as an element in attending the arts is missing, so some aspects of the school time performance are less than ideal.

By serving public audiences, children get to share experiences within their extended families. Mothers, fathers, siblings, grandparents, and best friends can go to the theatre together and share a special event that may resonate for years in the memory. Theatre attendance is here seen as family oriented. Children observe that their parents choose to spend their time and money on attending the theatre, and this is a life lesson missing from the school experience. But many adults do not place a priority on attending arts events. Children whose families do not choose the arts, for fiscal reasons or merely from lack of exposure, are denied any chance to experience the theatre for young audiences. It could be argued that both audiences should be served, but it is not always possible to do so with limited resources, as their needs are, in some ways, not compatible.

School audiences are more interested in the educational component of the production, although they also expect that the experience will be an enjoyable one, at least for the students. (Of course, repeat attendance is much easier to achieve if the teachers also find themselves enjoying the production.) Generally, teachers must justify trips to the theatre, or assembly programs that pull time away from the classroom, with some curricular objective. A play based on a title that the students read in class is an obvious attraction, but so are plays that relate to themes or units being taught in the same time frame that the production is offered. Rarely does a single class decide to take a field trip; more common is the decision to bring one or more whole grades, so a consensus must be forged among several teachers, usually with the support of the school administration. It is even more difficult at the older grades, because an English teacher who wants to bring a class to see a classic onstage is also pulling the students out of math or science class in order to make the field trip. Administrative support and lots of negotiation are common. Teachers need to be highly motivated in order to bring off such an experience for their students, or the theatre experience has to so clearly relate to specific goals of the school system that logic swings the argument towards a necessity to attend.

Marketing to school audiences is also completely different from reaching the general public. Teachers are inundated with paper, and tend not to notice advertising material placed in their mailboxes. Direct mail, radio, and television may be useful in raising background awareness, but does not often translate immediately into sales. Moreover, because of the lead time necessary to plan a field trip, word of mouth about a successful production is rarely effective. Brief presentations at faculty meetings early in the school year by staff or volunteers from the theatre can be a very effective tool to raise awareness of available productions and their relevance to the school curriculum. An arts coordinator among the teaching staff in each building is another great tool. This person can often hand-deliver printed season material, and point out which plays would be most relevant to the particular teachers. It may be wise to recruit such coordinators, giving them some incentive such as free tickets for their own classes. Nearly every teacher has an E-mail address, and many use this form of communication daily. Theatres should attempt to collect these addresses and send out regular bulletins of offerings, stressing their relationship to the school's needs. Another valuable marketing technique, which also gives an added value to the theatrical production, is to offer in-service workshops for teachers. Most districts require continuing education from their teachers, and theatre educators can offer useful techniques for classroom use of the arts. These can be tied to specific productions, and offered only to attending teachers; or they can be general arts-in-education workshops that raise the overall level of awareness and desire for arts experiences for their students. Printed or website curriculum guides for each production also offer teachers specific exercises to do before and after plays, and provide them with more justification for making those plays a part of their students' education.

Public audiences are more likely to attend the theatre because they expect to be entertained. Parents want to feel as though their children will be exposed to uplifting cultural experiences, but fun is a major requirement. This audience is also attracted by familiar titles, positive feedback from newspaper critics or family friends, clever publicity, and seasonal events like a play with a Christmas theme in December. Adults who have fond memories of a particular story may want to share it with the younger generation. Older children may attend the theatre to see familiar book titles, or even specific performers that they know. Teens respond to influence from their peers, so if one of their friends is enthusiastic about attending the theatre, a group may come along. For all ages, theatre can be part of a family outing, with a special meal at a favorite restaurant, or even as the featured event of a birthday celebration for one of the children. Special ticket prices for churches or drama clubs may also attract groups to weekend performances.

Marketing to this audience is very much like marketing any product to the general public. If it is possible to obtain mailing lists of households with children, direct mail is a very useful tool. Radio and television, though expensive, are also effective at reaching the family audience. Subscriptions can guarantee repeat attendance by loyal patrons, but selling subscriptions to families with different aged children is a particularly difficult task. Parents know that schedules are often disrupted by illness or school events and resist making plans too far ahead. If their children are spread out in age, they may not want to bring them all to the same plays, feeling that the younger ones will be bored by the plays for the older ones, and vice versa. Flexible packages like ticket coupon books or membership discounts may be a better way to attract repeat customers, without locking them into dates and times of performances far in the future. In many cases, the decision to attend the theatre is made only a few hours ahead of time, so a listing in daily event calendars in the local media is an essential sales tool. Competition for theatre attendance comes from movies, zoos and museums, amusement parks, sports and other outdoor events, or other family activities. Word of mouth is also a useful way to attract these audiences, but in order to be of any use, plays need to run over several weekends. It is wise to pack what subscribers you have into the first weekend, in order to allow them time to tell their friends about the show. Over time, theatres should work to build a reputation for excellence that will create demand for their tickets, and confer an aura of prestige on season subscribers.

At Stage One, during my tenure as producing director, our primary focus was the school-time bussed-in audience. Performances were given Monday through Friday, usually at 10:00 A.M., allowing for the school day to start and then busses to be loaded up for travel to the theatre. A second performance at noon was frequently possible, if the play did not exceed 75 or 80 minutes in running time, as the busses generally needed to be back at school by 2:00 P.M. to start taking children home. If the play was very short—say a Participation Play running about 55 minutes—the second show could start at 11:30. As we were operating as a resident company, often doing two or more shows in repertory, the actors' days fell into a consistent pattern: First call at 9:30 A.M.; shows at 10:00 A.M. and 12:00 P.M.; possible changeover to a different set for tomorrow's play; break from 2:00 to 3:00 P.M. and rehearsal for the next play from 3:00 to 6:00 P.M. Other than during final technical or dress rehearsals, the lives of the company fit into a normal working day. This was often an attraction to actors who wanted a degree of regularity. Over the years, many of them bought homes, married, and raised families of their own. That is, perhaps, not common for the American professional actor, who typically works a series of eight-week contracts at many different theatres, and rarely has evenings free if they are performing in a show.

By choosing to prioritize school audiences we made the selection of a season very dependent on curriculum concerns. We always needed to know what the classes were studying at each grade level. In fact, we created an advisory group of educators from the different school systems in our region, and met with them quarterly to track issues affecting the schools, as well as themes and stories of interest at the various age levels. This group also played a role in deciding which plays would be promoted to which ages. In keeping with our developmental theatre philosophy (see Chapters 8 and 9), we targeted specific grade levels for each of our productions. Discussing plots and themes with the advisory group helped to focus each production on the most suitable recipients. Educational materials to supplement the productions could also be tested with these educators, and were often improved by their comments and suggestions.

Since our primary audience of school children would be nearly homogenous in age, responses to the plays could also be more accurately predicted. An audience of all fourth and fifth graders, with a few teachers and chaperones scattered among them, is much more volatile and reactive than an audience of mixed ages or family groups would be (see Chapter 14). Although the artists must still consider the responses of the few adults in the audience, (and, indeed, their own artistic integrity,) when creating the production it is useful to know that it will be primarily school groups attending, as their more consistent reactions will affect the actors' timing and many other aspects of the performance. This type of audience tends to generate the most energy during a performance, and it can be both challenging and rewarding to the actors to be the recipients of that passion.

Many other TYA companies choose to focus their energies on the public audience. These companies tend to perform heavily on weekends, often scheduling two or three performances on Saturday, as well as one or two on Sunday. They may also offer early evening performances on school nights, at least for part of the week. Obviously, there are fewer time slots available for public presentations, and many other family activities compete in those periods, but the theatres that serve this audience are not locked in to the myriad of rules and bureaucratic procedures that govern school attendance. Theatres may also attract a different pool of artists by scheduling rehearsals in the evenings or on non-performance weekends. This, of course, allows their performers to pursue day time employment. It also makes it much easier to use child performers in age appropriate roles, as they are not in school during performance times. (On those occasions when a company like Stage One uses student performers, it is usually necessary to double cast the young roles, so the children could attend their own classes at least every other day.)

Choice of repertory when playing for primarily family audiences is obviously not dependent on school curriculum. Familiar titles are still easier to sell than unknown ones, but clever marketing that makes new work sound like compelling entertainment can bring in audiences willing to experience original stories, especially if the theatre has built a reputation for excellence in this area. By avoiding school time performances, length of the performance is also less of an issue. (See the next essay for a discussion of play length.) With the public, it is even possible to take an intermission, if the play's structure warrants it. (At school performances, Stage One occasionally allowed for 90-second stretch breaks in longer plays where an intermission would normally occur. It is not wise to allow younger school groups, from several different schools, to descend on the lobby en masse for an intermission. It would almost inevitably take a very long time to get them back into their seats.)

The aesthetics of playing to multiple ages simultaneously, such as a public family audience, has its own particular rewards. When playing to a mixed group, actors generally feel that all the elements of their performance are being appreciated by some portion of the audience. Adults follow the subtleties of the dramatic conflict, and laugh at sophisticated textual references, while the younger members of the audience may get bound up in the physical and emotional struggle to a greater extent. Different elements of the production appeal to different segments of the audience, and children and parents are given a rare opportunity to enjoy the same event, for different reasons, and observe each other in that enjoyment. Follow-up to the performance is less structured for families than for schools, but parents who want to can build family discussions around the shared event, and many families create their own traditions around heightened arts experiences. The theatre may also provide websites or handouts that promote parent/child activities, games, or discussion topics.

At Stage One, despite our orientation toward the schools, we also offered our productions to a public audience at a small number of weekend matinees. Although the seasons' titles were chosen primarily for marketing to educators, parents could bring their families, and even buy subscriptions, if their children were not being exposed through the schools. These performances, representing perhaps only 10% of our total performance, were satisfying for a number of reasons. It enabled those families that know and love the arts to participate as families. Sometimes, it enabled a child who had seen the play with his school to be the expert, and share the experience over again with his parents or siblings. It allowed for children outside the recommended grade level, but who had a strong interest in theatre to expand their access. It allowed children who went to nonparticipating schools, but whose parents were arts lovers, to be involved. It also gave the actors a chance to be seen by at least a few other adults, which often gave them a different sense of accomplishment than would be had by limiting their work to only students.

But public performances also presented administrative difficulties. There was sometimes a sense that we were competing against ourselves between the two audiences. Parents would often buy subscriptions, and later find out that their children were going to one of the plays that season with their schools. (This would be another reason to develop a membership or flexible coupon system instead of a fixed performance ticket system to promote multiple sales.) Titles that fit well into school themes were sometimes difficult to sell to families. In fact, the reputation that we had built up as an educational resource caused many in the community to assume that we *only* served schools, and we were often told by parents that they assumed we never did public shows, despite the many marketing attempts that were made to change this image. Of course, in all our public sales efforts, we were careful not to damage our image with the teachers, who provided, after all, 90% of our audience. Eventually, we realized that we needed two completely distinct marketing campaigns if we were to serve both audiences, and this placed considerable strain on our resources—both in terms of administrative personnel, and marketing funds.

In spite of these obstacles, I always felt that it was appropriate to try to augment our school performances with at least a few public offerings, if only because it opened up new sources of revenue for the theatre. While there are certainly many foundations and public and private sources of funding for school based activities, there were always a number of local corporations—wonderful corporate citizens of the community—who would give support to our organization only if the public was somehow included. Benefactors commonly expect recognition for their philanthropy, and activities during school hours were often below the radar screen in terms of the kinds of recognition desired. In addition, newspapers rarely review events that are exclusively for schools. Doing public performances was another way to get the local media to cover our work, which was an important source of feedback so that we could continually monitor our quality. This was an essential way to keep our programs visible, so that potential donors could stay aware of our needs and accomplishments. Of course, we were also able to charge more for tickets to public performances, and this helped to compensate for the artificially low ticket prices set for school admission.

The trade off between reaching potentially all of the children, and preserving more artistic freedom to explore wider boundaries, is one that must be examined vigilantly. Understanding the logistical and aesthetic requirements of both audiences and choosing carefully to meet the needs of one, or the other (or both, if feasible) is essential if the TYA is to communicate its vision to the community that supports it. It is also necessary for the individual artists involved to anticipate potential sources of frustration and possible feelings of externally imposed limits. These limits can only be accepted if the mission of the organization is compelling enough to provide satisfaction, and clearly communicated to all of the stakeholders.

18. THE 60-MINUTE MYTH

How long is a story?

Some events in our lives are timed events. The half-hour nightly news program on the television takes exactly 30 minutes, including commercials. If there is a lot of news that day, the program still lasts only 30 minutes. If absolutely nothing happened that was newsworthy, the program runs on for the same 30 minutes. Entertainment programs, like "sit-coms" or dramas, are also exactly an hour or a half-hour long. Many sports are timed, although variations in rules often allow for the clock to be stopped for various reasons. A football game is an hour, but since the clock stops when the ball goes out of bounds, or for many other reasons, the actual game may vary in length. A soccer game is ninety minutes and the clock never stops, except for the halftime break, but the referee has the discretionary power to add on time to compensate for injuries or other occurrences. And in most high schools and colleges, classes run for a fixed time, usually fifty minutes. All activities, lectures, exercises, discussions, etc., have to fit into a fifty-minute framework.

Other events are not timed. Baseball and tennis are two sports without clocks. The end of the game is determined by reaching a certain score, in the latter case, or by the number of outs made, in the former. Special rules prevent ties by extending the games further, if necessary. On television, a breaking news story of major importance may interrupt the pattern of timed shows. Such a program may go on as long as events continue to unfold. Its length is determined by its perceived relevance. And in most elementary schools, classroom events go on as long as the teacher thinks they are productive, switching activities when she senses that the children are losing their engagement with the current task.

A performing arts event is an untimed event. Although a symphony is generally considered a "major" piece of music, there is no prescribed length for one. An overture or a fanfare is expected to be a shorter piece of music, but there is no prescribed length for one of those either. In the theatre, there are short plays, so called "one-act" plays, and there are longer, "full-length" plays. A one-act cannot have an intermission, but a full-length play may also be performed without a break. And there is no set time limit on either category. A one-act can be ten minutes or ninety. A full-length play can be eighty minutes or four hours. (Note that a long one-act may even be longer than a short full-length play!) In Lewis Carroll's *Alice in Wonderland*, the rules for court trials are clearly set out by the King of Hearts: "Begin at the beginning, go on until you come to the end, and then stop!" And that is the rule for arts events, too.

But somehow, the rules for TYA plays got mixed up with the rules for class periods. Producers of plays for young audiences started believing that these plays must remain close to an hour in length, or they would not be successful. Schools embraced this concept, because it made their lives much easier. An assembly program with a visiting arts group could take up exactly one 50-minute period, and therefore not disrupt much of the day's schedule, or at worst, the next class would be a trifle shorter since the 10-minute break between class periods might also be absorbed by the program. This concept was for some reason carried over to arts field trips, although the students were already going to be out of school for much of the day. In fact, many schools seek out opportunities to do more than one thing when they are out of school on a field trip, in part to make the best use of the bus costs. They combine a play with a trip to a museum, or a local business, or a picnic, etc. For such an outing, the length of the play should be irrelevant, but the expectation that the play would be an hour long was somehow still maintained. Presenters of TYA plays that bussed in school groups began insisting on a 60-minute time limit. Playwrights succumbed and began to retool their artistic visions, compressing or expanding them—as if they were television shows—in order to make them all one homogenous length. Plays that were translated from other countries, where this concept of a time limit never got started, had also to be cut or extended to conform to the standard length. The actors' union, Equity, got so accustomed to the one-hour limit that they even wrote it into some of their contracts for the TYA. Publishers that wanted their work to be produced applied a clock standard to all submissions, and before we knew it, we were stuck with a mythological and arbitrary time for all our work in the TYA. To an artist, such an artificial yardstick should be unacceptable. How long is a story? How long should a play be?

There are several factors at work in the consideration of this issue. Some of these concerns are valid; others are less so. The first, and perhaps most pervasive, is the question of attention span. There is a popular notion that young children have short attention spans. But anyone who believes that is true has never watched an eight-year old playing ball with his friends outside when it starts to grow dark, or a ten-year old with an interesting video game, or a twelve-year old with a compelling novel, or any aged child at a really well made two-hour movie. These children have no problem staying on task. It takes a real effort sometimes to get them to stop what they are doing and eat a meal or brush their teeth at bedtime. In fact, the argument might be made that it is adults who have short attention spans. Adults have been conditioned by years of watching television to expect a commercial break every seven minutes or so. (There are other effects of technology on the brain, as well, such as an expectation that one can pause or rewind an onscreen action. That doesn't happen in the live theatre. See Chapter 7 for more on this phenomenon.) In any case, if you believe that a child has a short attention span, it would be logical to assume that it averages much *less* than 60 minutes.

One of the cornerstones in the educational philosophy of Maria Montessori is that children can concentrate on a task for a very long time. Schools that follow her methodology note that children will remain engaged for hours, especially if the child has chosen the activity without apparent direction or monitoring from an adult. Some educators would characterize the educational engineering in a Montessori school as benign neglect, but good teachers in other systems have also discovered that children will focus on tasks for an extensive period—if they are interested in them. Motivation is a contributor, probably the most important contributor, to attention span.

The question to ask is not how long a play for children should be, but rather what motivates children to watch a play, no matter how long it is? If the audience members believe in the verisimilitude of the characters; if they care what happens to them; if the story is interesting, and contains some variations in the story telling—now action-packed, now reflective; if the resolution seems appropriate to their developing standard of ethical justice; then they will stay absorbed for however long it lasts.

But occasionally at TYA plays, one sees an audience that appears restless or inattentive. In my forty plus years of writing, directing, and producing plays for all ages of children, I have identified some factors that consistently do seem to affect the attention given to the stage by children. Most of these are elements within the play that might bore them, or confuse them to the point where they assume that they are not supposed to understand something—a common event in the adult world; and one which children tolerate with varying degrees of acquiescence.

For example, music makes a vital contribution to the theatre. Incidental music makes connections and foreshadows emotional peaks. A song can also be valuable because it allows the character singing to explore or expand upon an emotional state or relationship while the action of the story slows down to allow for that introspection. But younger children (up to around age eleven) once they figure out what the emotional state is, typically do not like to stop and reflect on it while the chorus repeats itself. They are much more interested in what will happen next. I believe that songs and musical interludes in TYA should be carefully constructed so that they do their job, and then stop. Wallowing in an emotion or relationship is not something that children understand well. Once they get it, they get it. I would recommend that musical numbers be kept short, and avoid repetition merely for the sake of hearing a melody over again. A reprise reminds us of a relationship or emotion, and should usually be much shorter than the initial appearance of that song in the script. All songs should move the play forward and then end.

A similar case could be made against prolonging the denouement at the end of a play. Adults may like drawn out resolutions where all of the plot refinements get neatly wrapped up, but children are ready to stop when the principle action is resolved. The hero gets his reward, the villain gets punished, and the play is over. There are also interior scenes in adult plays where an action pauses while the participants reflect at great length on what it might mean. (Shaw's plays are filled with such scenes, delightfully drawn out with subtle humor.) Those moments are likely to puzzle or bore children; they usually want to get on with the action of the story.

Children are also apt to show restlessness at long scenes where ideas are discussed. They may recognize that the ideas are important to the characters, and so they may be willing to listen a little, but under the age of twelve or thirteen or so they are not yet fully accepting of the concept that the reason for doing something is just as important as what one does. Often they will react to such an extended moment in a play by wiggling. Wiggling is different from losing interest; in fact, it indicates an attempt to stay interested, but without a real understanding of why it is important. After a few moments of wiggling, young children might give up; at least until the next action that clearly moves the story forward. It might, however, be a positive thing to have one or two of these moments in a play. It provides something for the older children and adults, and teaches the younger audience members that there are ideas that their beloved characters find relevant. But if it goes on too long, it will feed the perception that children have short attention spans.

The inclusion of sub-plots in a play is another area that may confuse or bore young children. It can be done if the secondary story includes characters as compelling and worthy of empathy as the main plot, but if not, the moments when the main story isn't being advanced might create restlessness or inattention. For example, in several different productions of *The Wind in the Willows*, I have observed that the audience aged seven through ten gets very involved in Mole's story, and also in Toad's. They are completely absorbed in the action when either of those two characters operates. But when Badger appears and starts to reminisce about the good old days, they always wiggle a bit. They cannot quickly sense the connection to the characters they care about. Adults and teens attending love that scene, however, and it isn't too long, so I always leave it in for the reasons mentioned above.

Of course, the subject matter of the story may or may not appeal to children, depending on their age and experience. Observers may perceive that a play seems too long when, in fact, it is really just not very interesting because it is outside the audience's frame of reference or areas of interest. The story of *Tom Sawyer* is very appealing to upper elementary and middle school children, but may only frighten or confuse the primary grades. And high school students may feel that it is beneath them to be taken to see a title from a younger stage, now that they are "mature" young adults.

And then there is the issue of quality. A poorly acted play will seem much, much longer than a well acted one. That is true at every age level. If children can't hear, or can't understand, or don't care about the protagonist, then the play will seem like a punishment and not an exciting arts event. Of course, they will respond with inattention and boredom. Adults would also, except that they are more conditioned into being polite and suffering in silence.

Above all, to be really effective at holding the audience the script and the direction must include variety—for both children and adults this is important. Good playwrights know how to mix the energy flow of a play so that it creates a constant shifting between relaxation and tension. Action scenes are alternated with discussion or reflection. Long scenes are followed by short ones. And throughout the play there is a build to a climax, and then a speedy resolution. Directors know how to orchestrate these script variations into the rhythmic staging of the play. The right texture of changes within the structure of a play can maintain engagement for even a very young child. Many films for children do this well, and could be studied as a model.

These few tips and your own observations of what works and doesn't work onstage will help to secure the audience's engagement for the length of the play. However ensuring that the TYA play will hold their attention is only half of the battle. Ultimately, the producer or presenter of a play for young audiences has got to obtain the agreement of the school administrators and teachers that it will be just fine if the play runs 65 minutes, or 85, or even longer. This will require a strategy that goes beyond marketing – that anticipates the consumer's needs, and meets them. I have no prescription that will guarantee success. But I firmly believe that the issue might be resolved if the theatre manager can draw the educators into a conversation about the benefits of an untimed arts event. Of course, the manager must also demonstrate sensitivity to the real needs of the school, and two issues related to time always seem to be raised by the school administrators: A) the concern about length of time without access to restrooms, and B) the school bus schedule.

Addressing the first issue, it is certainly the prevailing custom that adult plays have intermissions, (although, increasingly, full-length plays without them are coming into vogue). Intervals actually serve several purposes. There are artistic purposes—allowing for complex set and costume changes, or allowing for the apparent passage of a long time in the action of the play; and/or administrative purposes—allowing for patrons to smoke a cigarette, make a phone call, or purchase something from the concession stand, thereby adding to the theatre's revenue, and, of course, time to use the restrooms,.

At public TYA performances, all of these rationales may apply. In fact, there are many adult plays to which children will be brought, and they will then observe all of the intermission rituals, just like their parents do. But it is rare to find an intermission at a school performance in the United States. Generally, there is more than one school group attending at a time, and therefore no single authority which can command the students. Teachers will be afraid that they will lose their charges in the melee of a mass restroom break. Older kids have been known to sneak off to smoke, which can make trouble for their chaperones. And concession sales are probably not a good idea at school shows since not all children have the same resources to make purchases, and if they did the intermission would stretch out to half an hour or more. In many European TYA companies, especially in the countries of Northern Europe: Scandinavia, Germany, Holland, Russia, etc; intermissions are taken, and the students seem to have a better understanding of intermission protocol. Perhaps that is because they have been trained to it, as the performing arts are more universally accepted as a part of the life of the community. At my own theatre, when the artistic requirement for an interval was pressing, we have often taken a ninety-second stretch break, in which the students were encouraged to stand up and stretch, but not leave the area of their seats. Students and teachers are always advised in advance that these breaks will occur—either in a curtain speech, or in advance materials, or both. If really necessary, a student in discomfort has been known to make the round trip to the bathroom in about ninety seconds.

At Stage One we once did a production of *Great Expectations* that ran 125 minutes without any intermission and only a few of the students left to use the facilities during the show. Once again, motivation can sometimes affect how long a child can wait to go to the restroom. We were also fortunate that our theatre architect had designed lightproof foyers behind each of the theatre doors, so that those children who did leave and return could get in and out without affecting the lighting of the production. Physical discomfort will eventually prevent an audience member from enjoying even the best production, however. Fortunately, many of the concerns expressed above (short songs, lack of sub-plot, etc.) also act to shorten the TYA play. A typical running time at Stage One was more often 70-90 minutes for the older grades, and 55-70 minutes for the younger, whose stories tend to be more quickly told. As school administrators become more informed as to the real requirements of the art form, they frequently are surprised to discover that their children are capable of much more lengthy engagement than they had anticipated. Indeed, that is one thing the arts can sometimes teach the schools.

The second issue—school bus schedules—is harder to solve. The busses have to pick up children from their homes and take them to the schools. In some districts they have to make a double run, taking the secondary students to school, and then starting over with the elementary age group. The end of the day is the reverse. They are therefore only available for field trip transportation in a very narrow window. Distance from the school to the theatre is then a factor, with some driving over 30 or 40 minutes to reach their destination, and the same to return. There must also be time allowed to unload the bus, and move the students into their seats, and then at the end of the play, move them back out to the busses. Depending on the size of the theatre and the availability of skilled ushers (see Chapter 19) this can take as much as 30 minutes on each end. In most school districts, the time slot available for actual performance is then only from around 9:45-10:00 A.M. to about 1:15-1:30 P.M., or only about 3 ½ hours, with a little grace period perhaps -- necessary for traffic delays, bad weather etc. It can be seen from these numbers that a single performance can be almost any length and fit into the day, but a theatre that wishes to schedule double performances back to back must concern itself with the length of the play. At Stage One, choosing to perform a longer play became, then, a budgetary issue, as we were committing to doing only one show a day. (On one or two occasions, we were able to move a lengthy production into a much larger theatre, where doing only one performance a day did not entail a sacrifice in the number of students we could serve, or in income.) With plays up to 90 minutes in length, two performances could usually be squeezed into a day, although that does require efficient ushers, and starting on time.

I would love to see the question of a play's length become a non-issue. For this to happen in most communities, theatre managers will need to enter into an honest dialogue with school administrators. It may be the role of the arts to push back barriers and open up new vistas of experience, and nowhere is that a more appropriate mission than when dealing with the arts for young people. Setting arbitrary time limits on a theatrical event is certainly a barrier that needs to be removed. But schools have real issues, such as bus schedules, and these will need to be factored into a theatre's planning. Every community will have slightly different concerns, and every problem must be solved by the people involved. But it must be begun by asking the right questions, and then listening to the answers. Once educators are made to realize that the live performing arts have a different time imperative than do television programs, and a different aesthetic, then they can be engaged to help to solve the problem. After all, they are choosing to bring their students to the arts because they believe in their enduring values. And one of those values involves the creation of a world in which time defines itself not through a clock but through a story.

19. THE FIELD TRIP AND THE HOUSE MANAGER

"Today is the big day! My class is going to see the play at Stage One. My parents signed the permission slip for me to go—everybody in the class got permission. The teacher has been preparing us with special assignments, and we even drew pictures of what we thought the stage setting might look like. Right after the second bell rings, we will get on the school bus and head to the theatre. I hope I get to sit with my best friend. I am so excited!"

The theatre staff is excited, too. We have been rehearsing, building the scenery and costumes, developing the curriculum guides for the teachers, marketing the play, and taking the bookings. The production is ready for the audience, and we have sold a lot of tickets. But there is one area over which the theatre's artistic staff has limited control, and it may be the particular feature that determines whether the play is a success or not. Almost overlooked in our preparations is the journey that the audience takes to and from their seats. We hope that the performance will be inspiring, and that nothing will detract from the aesthetic experience. But, in truth, the bus ride from the school to the theatre, the way the students are moved from the bus into their seats, the environment of the theatrical space, and the return journey to the school are all important components of the audience member's experience on that special day. Theatre producers must do everything in their power to insure that the play is well served by that journey.

The journey usually starts with a bus ride. One or two theatres actually have their own busses, or at least contracts with busses to bring students on field trips. In larger cities, students may also come on public transportation, which is generally the most common method used in European cities. But in the USA, most field trips are initiated by the schools. They either own or contract bus transportation, and in many cases it is a major portion of their annual budgets. In the narrow time window between dropping off the final load of children at their school for the day, and picking up the first load for the trip home, the busses are commonly made available for field trips. If the teachers have remembered to schedule them, and if they had no major traffic or mechanical problems during their morning runs, they will show up at the school on time, and the classes will eagerly file down the hall and onto the bus. Leaving school in the middle of the day is automatically an adventure, so the students will already be energized. Depending on the advance curriculum materials provided by the theatre and the individual teacher's choice of whether or how to use those materials, the children are knowledgeable about the upcoming arts experience, or just excited to be getting out of school.

The theatre's first chance to make a good impression comes as the buses arrive at the front door. Hopefully, the bus drivers have been given clear instructions on where to pull up for the unloading process. The procedure we used at Stage One was implemented by paid house managers and volunteer ushers affiliated with our home base, the Kentucky Center for the Arts, and involved the use of *two* house managers. One of them was always on the street to greet the busses. No sooner had they arrived, but that manager was making his way onto the bus to say hello, to identify which group it was (quickly informing the inside house manager via headset so they could be checked off of the attendance list and directed to the proper seats), giving instructions to the teachers and students in a friendly manner, and making sure the bus driver knows where to park and when to return. From this first contact, it is essential that the groups be made welcome. Unless they stay after the play for a talk-back session or a tour, the only interpersonal contacts that the children will have on this field trip are *not* going to be with the artists; they are going to be with the house staff. If the staff sees the students as one more workplace irritation—probably chewing gum that they will get on the floor or seats—such an attitude will instantly be communicated to the children and teachers. If the manager who comes on to the bus seems happy to see the group, and handles them with respect and friendliness, his action will also inform the

BUSINESS: THE FIELD TRIP AND THE HOUSE MANAGER

audience that they are honored guests, and will be well treated. They will usually respond in kind with their best behavior.

As producing director, I always considered it very important to impress on the house managers and ushers my personal belief that their role was a critical part of our success. There were perhaps six or seven house managers who alternately handled the school matinee assignments, and there was a very large pool of ushers, some there only once or twice a month. Those volunteers were the people who actually seated the children. Not being able to meet with all of them individually, I designed a simple handout, which the house managers could post or give to their crew each day. In it, I tried to summarize what I was hoping for in terms of an interaction between them and the individual audience members. The following is the message of my handout:

I   see   you
I   C   U

I	C	U
N	O	N
V	N	D
I	T	E
T	R	R
E	O	S
	L	T
		A
		N
		D

At the top was the most important suggestion. Look at each child! Look them in the eyes. Let them know that you see them. One problem I have noticed whenever adults are moving children around they tend to treat them like a group instead of as individuals. Whether you think of it as "establishing rapport," or just as recognizing them as individuals, this is the most critical phenomenon. "I see you" becomes "ICU," which is a mnemonic reminder of the three behavioral patterns I wanted the ushers to exhibit. First, be friendly and *inviting*. Welcome the students into the theatre building and their own row and seat. They are the reason we perform the plays, so Invite them in.

Second, be in *control*. Know exactly where you want them to go, and where to sit. Direct them with authority. After all, you have moved thousands of students into their seats. Usually, there is a seating chart made up in advance by the theatre's booking manager and the house managers. At the Kentucky Center, a system has been devised to move the young people efficiently to their assigned space. One usher leads the group to the front row of the section they are to sit in. The second usher goes into the row behind that one, and as the line of students enters the first row, the second usher, from behind, moves them down to the last seat, and shows them that it is theirs. Quickly moving back towards the first usher, the second one places a student in each seat. The first usher controls the number of students who enter the row. When the second usher gets back to the first usher, they move up one row, and repeat the process. If the ushers are in control, it works very fast, and lets the audience feel confident that they are being well cared for by a team that knows what they are doing. This has the additional benefit of immediately letting the teachers know that the house staff is in charge. The teachers are then free to relax and enjoy the show with their students.

The third key behavior is to *understand* the audience. This refers especially to understanding the differences in experience and expectations between age groups. Teens cannot stand to be treated as children; preschoolers will not move as quickly as middle school students. The ushers need to adjust their rhythm and attitude to the particular group they are escorting. With experience, they will learn how to make this adjustment. Pairing an inexperienced volunteer with a veteran is a good way to get them started in the acquisition of this understanding. It is good to remember that this place is unfamiliar to the children. They may be confused; they may even be a little bit afraid. That look in the eyes, necessarily brief, can let the usher know which child may need a little bit of extra time.

Between leaving the bus and meeting the ushers who are to seat them, the students will be entering the lobby of the theatre. Hopefully, they will have a second or two to confirm the sense that they are not in school anymore. If you are fortunate enough to perform in a real theatre space, give the children a chance to appreciate it as they enter. If there is visual art, point it out. If there are other amenities, a restaurant or gift shop, that can be used, perhaps on another visit when they are with their parents, let them know. Anything that can make the field trip a special event will help reinforce the impact of the actual performance. There may also be groups entering from other schools. Instill some pride in the group you are escorting. Let them know that "*their* school is always well behaved and looked up to by others". Of course, this is also a good time to point out the location of the restrooms, particularly if the school is some distance away and they have been on the bus for an extended time. If that is the case, it may be better to let them use the facilities before seating the group. During this transition time between the street and the theatre, one representative from each school will be checking in at the box office, completing payment, verifying numbers, etc. Sometimes handouts are given to the check-in teacher, such as printed theatre programs, or stickers to be worn by the students after the show proclaiming, "I went to the Kentucky Center," or some such message designed to boost parental involvement. If this happens, it is necessary to remind the teacher to distribute them only after the children are back on the bus.

Once all of the students are seated, there are still some steps that must be taken to ensure a good experience for all. The most important is to make sure that there is an usher on duty inside the theatre at all times. This is a basic safety concern. In the unlikely event of an emergency of some kind—a sick child or a tornado warning, for example—there needs to be someone in attendance who is trained to take charge. The presence of an authority figure does not relieve the teachers of the need to monitor their own students, but it does reinforce the idea that the theatre staff is there to insure a safe and enjoyable experience for all.

In my many years of experience, students rarely misbehave at performances. They may enter the theatre feeling like escaped prisoners and ready to cause trouble, but once the play starts they are usually drawn in. On those rare occasions when an individual or a small group has determined in advance to cause a public disturbance and make rude comments, or throw coins or other objects at the stage, the visible usher will act as a restraint. This individual may solicit the help of the adult chaperones, as needed. The last resort in case of true misbehavior is to raise the house lights, at least to a glow. Once the anonymity provided by darkness is removed, the anti-social behavior will usually stop. Or, if not, at least the perpetrators can be easily identified and disciplined. When this type of rowdiness happens, it almost always has nothing to do with the performance, but is a planned act of rebellion by a particular individual or small group. (More general restlessness, leading to an ultimate loss of interest in the performance, is different—that is usually caused by a lack of quality in the production. Children may go back and forth to the restroom constantly, and there will be a lot of talking to their neighbors. Neither the performers nor the teachers will be satisfied with that type of experience. In such cases, the ushers will really be tested, but still must act to protect the safety of the audience.)

In our theatre we always had a brief curtain speech before the play started. The actors' union, Equity, requires that an announcement be made prohibiting photographs and/or recordings. We added a reminder to turn off cell phones and beepers. This was also an opportunity to thank a particular sponsor, or recognize a particular group in attendance. The same information is usually given by the house manager meeting the bus on the street, but some groups come in cars or public transportation and so miss the first contact. Another use of the pre-show speech is to remind the students to remain seated after the performance, so that they may be dismissed in an orderly fashion, by groups.

Following the speech, which may be live or recorded (if recorded it is best given after bringing the house lights to half strength, so as to signal the audience to listen) the house lights dim, and the play begins. If all goes well, the journey of the audience's imagination has begun. For the next period of time, identification and empathy will take them out of themselves and the daily life of the school. When the action of the play is resolved, the actors come back on stage for a curtain call, which is our chance to express our appreciation by applause. Children have to be taught the function of a curtain call. They will usually assume that there is another scene to the play; so if they are inexperienced, it will be the teachers' job to start the clapping. By their second or third trip to the theatre, the children have caught on and are quick to cheer loudly for their favorites.

When the play ends, the inside house manager comes onto the stage with a microphone and reinforces the audiences response to the play. By then, the house manager on the street is able to report via headset the order in which the busses are lined up out front, and the inside manager can dismiss the groups in exactly the right order. If a group has made arrangements to meet the actors for a talk-back session, backstage tour, or workshop, they would remain in the theatre. If a group has made a special request for a space to eat their picnic lunch (either inside the Center, or on the grass nearby) they can be escorted to that spot by an usher. If there is another performance that day, the house staff instantly shifts to bringing in the second group. The students and teachers are efficiently led back to their buses, and return to school, hopefully discussing the play or sharing their favorite moments on the journey home. This opportunity for the teachers to begin the follow-up process, perhaps with a group discussion, should not replace a more structured, thoughtful analysis once they are back in the classroom, but it is a good time for the students to dissect the experience in their own way, and at their own pace.

Although the TYA Company cannot have compete control over the process of getting the audience to and from the theatre––teachers, chaperones, ushers, and bus drivers are in charge of this phase of the experience—it is still a good idea to plan for the success of these caregivers. They are the ones who put the children in the seats, and who are responsible for them before and after the play. Enlist them as allies, and consider their needs and issues. The objective, after all, is to have eager young minds in the theatre seats ready to enjoy the play with no distractions. Then the theatre is free to do its job of transporting them on a journey to another world.

20. THE NEXT WAVE

Many generations of human beings have survived without the theatre for young audiences. Many children alive today somewhere

on the planet will never see a play produced especially for them—
—in fact they may never see a play at all—and the human race
will struggle on anyway. In a world beset by terrorism and civil
war and famine and disease one could make the case that TYA is
not really critically important to our well-being as a species. But
I disagree. Perhaps we can survive without the arts in our lives,
but doing so diminishes us, and makes our lives just that—about
survival. Our goal—our purpose in living at all—should be more
than just existence. It should be to reach our fullest potential
as human beings, and to help others to do the same. With the
arts—with the theatre—we can do much more than merely
survive. We can dream; we can imagine a better world; and we
can act so as to accomplish it. We can feel kinship with our fellow
creatures. We can begin to understand the condition of other lives
besides our own, and that should make us want to reach out to
those others and communicate meaningfully with them. We can
set goals for ourselves, and strive to reach them. We can express
joy and sadness, and join forces with all those before us who have
experienced those feelings, and endeavored to express them. We
can know the power of creativity, which is for me that aspect of
humanity that most renders us creatures of godliness.

Desiring, as I do, to see every child exposed in some way to the
magical transformative power of the theatrical art, I issue here
a call for leadership. The TYA needs artists, and managers, and
educators, and donors, and community visionaries to give it life,
and energy, and guidance, and watch it bloom. Where will they
come from?

My own dedication to TYA came from a pairing of two
passions—a love of children and a love of theatre. Others in the
field share my dual interests, in some cases discovering that they
did so only after they became parents themselves, and rededicating

their artistry to serving their children's generation. Many of us also feel as though we have something important to say to young people. Partly, it is our way of continuing to shape the world after we ourselves are gone. "Life is short; art is long," goes the ancient saying. Perhaps a calling to the TYA field is a quest for a certain kind of immortality. I suspect that I, and many others who dedicate themselves to serving children, might be partly motivated by such a drive.

On the other hand, I know of others who had no interest or intent to do this work and accidentally discovered the field. They were embarked on a career in theatre —intending to be Broadway stars, or serious Shakespearean artists. They took one job in the TYA—for experience, or money to pay off college loans, or to get a union card—and were surprised to find themselves responding to the love and energy flowing from the young audience at an emotionally satisfying theatrical event. The work itself appealed to the artist within them. Suddenly they realized that they had an unparalleled opportunity to grow as an artist, to play a wide range of roles, or to design a wide range of visual worlds. They have been given a different kind of recognition than that they initially expected to find. It is not fame, in the traditional sense of the word; and it is certainly not money. Rather it is recognition of their contributions as exceptional members of a community. Their colleague artists, their audiences, the parents and teachers of their audiences, the general public, and they themselves develop an appreciation for their unique role as the artist—the storyteller who brings the cultural heritage and ethical values of the society to the future citizens of the community. Years later, they begin to understand that they have embarked on a career with far more impact than mere stardom.

Still others in the field choose to participate in the full spectrum of the American Theatre, and can cross back and forth from one type of theatre to another. Perhaps they understand better than most how the future of that broad American Theatre is to be determined, for without knowledgeable new audiences graduating from the TYA and seeking a diverse set of theatre offerings, there will be much less demand for theatre in the adult sector. The European model is often one in which the same actors, directors, and playwrights work back and forth in the adult and TYA companies, and this brings a certain credibility to the field, since they are clearly among the better artists of their community, and have the ability to choose where to devote their energies. That they frequently choose the TYA indicates that they value it. From the TYA point of view, it can be very rewarding to include regular guest appearances by artists who are not solely identified with the field. It keeps us from becoming insular or complacent as to the quality of our work, it brings in fresh ideas and energy, and it opens up channels of communication into the "mainstream" adult theatre world.

Another continuing source of artistry and leadership is the world of universities and colleges. Despite cutbacks over the last decade, there are still a few excellent training programs in higher education that guide theatre students into TYA. Hopefully, graduates from these programs understand the educational implications of the work as well as the artistic ones. But learning how to make art in a university program is often dependent on how the teaching is accomplished. You must learn to make theatre by making theatre, not by studying how others have done it. My philosophy of teaching is very close to Galileo's when he said, "You cannot teach a man anything; you can only help him find it within himself." I think of teaching—especially if one is teaching an artistic skill, like playwriting or directing—as resembling the designing of an obstacle course. If I, as the teacher, design the course correctly, the muscles you, the student, develop in running through the course will be the muscles you need to perform the tasks ahead of you for the rest of your career. But each student must find his or her own way through the course, and there is always more than one way to get past each separate obstacle. Such a program develops unique artists and managers– – not reproductions of the professor. Happily, the better college programs keep turning out such contributors; graduates of some of these programs have made important contributions to the field; and more are entering it every year.

Perhaps most importantly, many of the future leaders of the TYA field in the USA are now developing within the staffs of the existing companies. As producing director of Stage One, it was always my philosophy to look first within the organization for talented individuals ready to move up in responsibility and position. Institutions, as institutions, have strengths and weaknesses. One of their strengths is clearly that they serve as breeding grounds for future leadership. During my twenty-five year tenure in Louisville, there were four different times when I designated one of our staff members as associate director, and half of those individuals went on to become artistic directors of companies – one of them of Stage One, when I ultimately moved on from there. (The other two went on to leadership positions outside of the professional theatre.) At the time I left, I was also serving as manager, and an individual who had been working for many years in a series of positions within the company took over as managing director, too. In a sense, I engineered my own retirement over a period of three years—with full cooperation and agreement from the board of directors—gradually transferring responsibilities to the two chosen successors.

Transitions to new leadership are always difficult times for an institution. Doing it from within, as we did at Stage One, can be seamless, and almost guarantees continuity for all the key staff and major programs—although the new leadership will, of course, gradually evolve the company in line with their own personal vision. I have usually found such measured transitions to be the easiest on all of the theatre's stakeholders. Even within the board csommittee structure, I always wanted there to be a vice-chair for every committee—so continuity was assured when any chairperson stepped down from that role.

The other method of replacing leadership—especially an artistic director—is to do a national search and bring in a relatively unfamiliar person from outside. This approach does have one advantage. It forces the institution to reexamine its mission and even its very existence. Transitions from within assume that we believe we are on track, and want to continue with slight course adjustments. External transitions confront the very real prospect of rethinking the company's direction. Whoever comes in is going to bring a very different corporate culture and personal vision than the person who is leaving. This may result in changes in support staff positions, and even in program. On certain occasions, of course, that may be exactly what an established company needs.

Long before companies reach the stage of becoming institutions, they must be started up by someone. New TYA companies regularly come into existence, generally summoned forth by the energies and commitment of a dynamic individual or well-connected group. It may be an artist who wants to start a company to explore his or her own creative contributions to a new—as yet nonexistent—audience. It may be a collective of artists who want to continue an association begun, perhaps, as students together in a college program. Another pattern involves an adult regional theatre that wants to ensure a future audience, so they began a corollary program of performances for young people, perhaps utilizing their apprentices as performers, or starting up a separate TYA company that plays on tour or in a second space. (A few of the more committed adult theatres have actually decided to program family plays regularly on their mainstage seasons.) Or it may be a college theatre department that wants to offer an active TYA to boost its relationship with the community. Or, perhaps, it is a community leader, a politician, or a group with a passion for the arts that notices how other cities have strong TYA companies, and their own does not. A combination of pride in the local "quality of life" and a genuine concern for giving something of value to the community's children is frequently the motivation for a board initiated theatre venture. To be successful, the artists with an inspiration to begin a company need to find supportive voices within their community. To be successful, the trustee driven model needs to find an artistic leader with a matching vision. Together, these two forces can build an enduring company that will serve millions of young people. Or, if the funding isn't there, or the artistic vision flawed, or perhaps if the chemistry is just wrong, the venture will sputter on for a while and then die. The ultimate losers, of course, are the children who do not get to have their very own theatre.

If the field of American TYA is in fact, a field, then it is still a relatively young one. Other than a few random plays that clearly held some interest for families, or a scattering of performances by child performers which were generally aimed at adult audiences, there was no such thing as a theatre for young audiences until the early 1900's. Mark Twain was a champion of the concept early in its existence, and in an often-quoted letter written in 1908, he said, among other things: "It is my conviction that the children's theatre is one of the very, very great inventions of the twentieth century." In a matter of a hundred years, it has grown in this country from nonexistence into a dozen or more fine professional companies of world class artistry, and many others aspiring to achieve that level of excellence. There are also many youth companies and process-oriented drama programs that inspire millions of young people as creators and performers. Classroom activities in the arts are at the core of many school programs, although they still struggle to find funding and support from the educational leadership of the nation. Teachers and parents who once share a truly magical theatre experience with their children are almost invariably transformed into life-long advocates of quality TYA.

The survival of this field seems guaranteed, although, of course, there will always be struggles, as programs destined for children—in fact our dedication as a nation to the very concept of childhood—should never be taken for granted. Beginning teachers frequently talk about their reason for becoming teachers, and remembering one great teacher somewhere in their past is often a major reason for their calling. I like to believe that somewhere in an audience today there sits a child who is destined to become one of the great leaders of the TYA movement of the future. That child will be so moved by the experience of today's performance that it will reshape his or her life, and instill a desire to give just that kind of experience to other children in the future. When you see me sitting towards the side of the theatre, glancing away from the stage and watching the children watching the performance, you can assume I am looking out for such a prospect. Led by future waves of passionate artists, managers, educators, donors, and visionaries the theatre for young audiences will be continued....

MOSES GOLDBERG

Moses Goldberg retired in March of 2003 after twenty-five years as Producing Director of Stage One: The Louisville Children's Theatre. He has also served as Artistic Director of the Asolo Touring Theatre and PAF Youth Theatre Center (Huntington, Long Island), and has directed professionally at theatres from Washington to Florida.

As a playwright, over twenty-five of his plays have been produced professionally, and ten of them have been published, including *Aladdin, The Outlaw Robin Hood, The Men's Cottage,* and *The Wind in the Willows.*

In 1990, Goldberg received the Charlotte B. Chorpenning Cup for his outstanding contributions to dramatic literature; and his textbook, *Children's Theatre: a Philosophy and a Method,* has been used in many of the nation's colleges and universities.

Active in the International Association of Theatre for Children and Young People *(ASSITEJ)*, Goldberg has attended meetings of the Association all over the world and directed the world premiere of Gennadi Mamlin's *On the Edge* at Moscow's famed Taganka Theatre.

He has taught at Florida State University and Southwest Texas State University and is frequently an adjunct faculty member at the University of Louisville and Hanover College.

He has been honored with the 2002 Governor's Artist Award for the state of Kentucky, and the 2005 Medallion of the Children's Theatre Foundation.